INTRODUCING

Heidegger

Jeff Collins • Howard Selina

Edited by Richard Appignanesi

Icon Books UK   Totem Books USA

This edition published in the UK
in 2007 by Icon Books Ltd.,
The Old Dairy, Brook Road,
Thriplow, Cambridge SG8 7RG
email: info@iconbooks.co.uk
www.introducingbooks.com

Sold in the UK, Europe, South Africa
and Asia by Faber and Faber Ltd.,
3 Queen Square, London WC1N 3AU
or their agents

Distributed in the UK, Europe, South
Africa and Asia by TBS Ltd., TBS
Distribution Centre, Colchester Road,
Frating Green, Colchester CO7 7DW

This edition published in Australia
in 2007 by Allen & Unwin Pty. Ltd.,
PO Box 8500, 83 Alexander Street,
Crows Nest, NSW 2065

Previously published in the UK and
Australia in 1998 under the title
Heidegger for Beginners, and in 1999
under the current title

This edition published in the USA
in 2007 by Totem Books
Inquiries to Icon Books Ltd.,
The Old Dairy, Brook Road,
Thriplow, Cambridge
SG8 7RG, UK

Reprinted 2006

Distributed to the trade in the USA by
National Book Network Inc.,
4501 Forbes Boulevard, Suite 200,
Lanham, Maryland 20706

Distributed in Canada by
Penguin Books Canada,
90 Eglinton Avenue East, Suite 700,
Toronto, Ontario M4P 2Y3

ISBN: 978-1840467-12-3

Originating editor: Richard Appignanesi

Printed by Gutenberg Press, Malta

BEGINNING WITH A QUESTION ...

"Is" is one of the most commonplace words in the English language. It slips into sentences almost unnoticed. It is difficult to speak, write or think without it.

But few people ask –

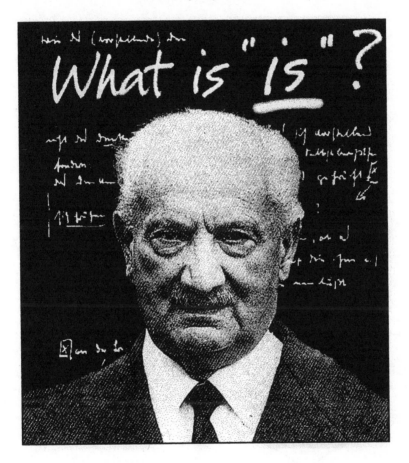

To the philosopher **Martin Heidegger** (1889-1976), that neglect was astonishing.

It is not just the neglect of a word, but of every resonance that such a word might have.

What is Being ?

" *Is*" is part of the verb "*to be*", the verb of being. To ask " What is *'is'* ? " is to ask a question of BEING. That was Heidegger's central preoccupation.

A strange concern? Heidegger proposed something extraordinary.

> *Western thought has FORGOTTEN to question being, not just recently, but in a process of neglect spanning 2,500 years.*

Heidegger's task: to return to the question. How could "being" be understood?

Was it possible to forge a **new disposition** towards "being", redirecting the trajectories of the last two millennia?

To Heidegger, what was at stake was nothing less than Western thought as it has been known – not only its philosophy, but its natural sciences, its human sciences, its everyday discourses.

To turn towards "being" meant: to turn away from their traditional concerns, to place their methods, their concepts and their underlying assumptions in question.

It means to propose a "thinking" that proceeds otherwise...

Few philosophers have proposed such a radical disturbance of philosophy.

It took Heidegger into some strange and contentious territories, both conservative and revolutionary, secular and theological, anti-traditional but deeply rooted, backward-looking while proposing a *future* thinking whose contours are still not settled.

Which Heidegger?

Unsurprisingly, the author "Heidegger" has been read in many different ways. It has often been said, there are *many* Heideggers.

● A Heidegger of German idealist philosophy, preoccupied with abstruse but fundamental questions of time, death, and the underlying anxiety or *Angst* of human living ...

● A scholarly Heidegger, "central to European philosophy", intersecting major currents of 20th century thought, interrogating philosophy's "great traditions" ...

● A theological Heidegger, taken to have offered a philosophical foundation for modern Christian thought ...

● ... and some Heideggers who disclaim this: one thoroughly *secular*, and another of *post*-theology, responding to the "death of God" while searching out what remains of religious thought in mystic traditions, Eastern religions, etc.

Against Heidegger

Not far away is a Heidegger of abstruseness, opacity, impenetrability and obscurity: the *bête-noir* of Anglophone "analytical" philosophy; a Heidegger of "dangerously unaccountable speculations"; of mysticisms and obfuscations; sham tautologies and self-important immersion in self-generated problems ...

The question of being? A senseless querying of what must be an absolute presupposition. If treated as a question there is no way of answering it ... Heidegger has displays of surprising ignorance, unscrupulous distortion and what can fairly be described as charlatanism.

British analytic philosopher A.J. Ayer in 1982

Heidegger's writings contain the last despairing glimmer of German romantic philosophy. His major work *Being and Time* is formidably difficult – unless it is utter nonsense, in which case it is laughably easy. I am not sure how to judge it, and have read no commentator who even begins to make sense of it.

British conservative philosopher Roger Scruton in 1992

For Heidegger

Heidegger has been interpreted more positively.

● ... the rescuer of PHENOMENOLOGY (a philosophy of **consciousness**) from its own self-constructed limits.

● ... contributor to modern HERMENEUTICS (the philosophical inquiry into how we make **interpretations**), crucial to the key hermeneutic theorist, Hans-Georg Gadamer.

● ... the most profound influence on 20th century EXISTENTIALISM and major figures like Maurice Merleau-Ponty and Jean-Paul Sartre.

● ... a POST-STRUCTURALIST Heidegger, coming before the name, anticipating the most innovative developments in philosophy and theory in recent decades – and a powerful formative influence even on thinkers who took other paths.

Jürgen Habermas ...
Herbert Marcuse ...
Michel Foucault ...

and many others.

● ... And a Heidegger of DECONSTRUCTION, providing the most important resource for its leading proponent, Jacques Derrida.

A Social Heidegger

There are Heideggers of social and cultural critique ...

● The Heidegger opposed to the conditions of MODERN INDUSTRIAL SOCIETY, its "mass" culture and technological modes of thought ...

● ... correspondingly, a Heidegger of conservative RURALISM, rooted in a vision of the "agrarian past"; its traditional modes of life and its assured lore and customs ...

● A proto-ECOLOGICAL Heidegger, offering a platform for "deep ecology": ways of thinking other than those of "exhaustive extraction and relentless appropriation"...

A Future Heidegger

There are figures of the **as-yet-unknown** Heidegger ...

● A substantial amount of Heidegger's large output remains unpublished. He lent a hand in setting up a Collected Edition, the *Gesamtausgabe,* in 1974. But the task of editing and publishing is far from complete. This is a "not-as-yet Heidegger", still awaited.

● Heidegger's personal papers are held in the German Literary Archive in Marbach, but access has been strictly limited ...

– A *private* Heidegger, mostly sealed from view.

Heidegger and Nazism

"Heidegger" is therefore a noun with many possibilities, and its arrival has often sparked controversies. The most fiercely argued issue has been Heidegger's involvement with Nazism.

Curiously, this has become a powerful reason for reading him. At issue are the *politics* of philosophy – the political forces at work on it and in it, its attachments and responsibilities.

For many readers, this is not a purely historical concern. It is bound up with our responses to resurgent nazisms now, emerging with new names and without a swastika in sight.

There are many figures of the "political" Heidegger ...

Heidegger was an energetic supporter of German National Socialism in the 1930s and never fully retracted or renounced his publicly-stated views.

● Was this a temporary career compromise – a Heidegger pressured by circumstances, perhaps politically misled?

● Or was it something deeper and more pervasive, something intimately bound up with his philosophy? That is another Heidegger: a thinker of **conservative revolution**, forging a discourse of "romanticism and steel", bound into a vision of regenerated primordial Germanness.

Whether philosophical or theological, socio-economic or political; none of these figures is totally unambiguous. Many are incompatible, and all are contentious.

But the most persistent figure is Heidegger as the "philosopher of being". What can this mean? *Is* there any question about being? How could any such question be cast, let alone answered?

13

Existence in a World of Things

"Being" might seem an innocuous site of inquiry, scarcely likely to upset the usual orders of the world. And it seems strictly **philosophical**, something rarefied and abstract; a soaring generality, perhaps invented uniquely by and for philosophers.

Indeed the word "being" might be so abstract, that meaning drops away from it ...

It's an empty word, fated to a hollow resonance...

*Doesn't it refer to existence in general, therefore to **everything**? After all, everything **exists**...*

*That is the wrong kind of approach. My task is to **find** a way of thinking "being" and a language in which to speak it.*

Nothing in particular has been identified...

Heidegger's sources, modes, methods and procedures – and his concepts and his vocabulary – were not going to be commonplace.

But why is "being" so troublesome? We deal every day with things that "exist"; whether mirrors or clouds, CDs or sonatas, or rain and cities.

Heidegger wanted to create a new awareness of that. And the awareness that might arise of this elusive "is-ness" will not be of the ordinary orders.

What could such an awareness be like?

As a first resort, *literature* might help: for instance, the writings of **Rainer Maria Rilke** (1875-1926), German poet and prose writer, and one of Heidegger's preferred authors.

Strange Moments

Rilke tried often to write of the strange moments in which the very fact of existence – that there *is* something – seemed to make itself felt.

In "Concerning the Poet" (1912), Rilke's poet-narrator takes a ferry from the Greek island of Philæ towards the open sea. Almost nothing happens. But Rilke is not interested in *events* of the usual narrative kind. His happenings are of a different order.

I had the rowers facing me, sixteen of them. Mostly their eyes saw nothing, their open gaze going out into the air …

…But sometimes I could catch one of them deep in thought, meditating on the strange disguised phenomenon facing him and on possible situations which might disclose its nature …

… when noticed, he immediately lost his strenuously thoughtful expression, for a moment all his feelings were in confusion, then, as quickly as he could, he reverted to the watchful gaze of an animal …

…until the beautiful serious expression became again the usual silly baksheesh* face, with its foolish readiness to assume any required humiliating distortion of thanks.

* a gratuity, tip or alms

Rilke's concerns are styled like Heidegger's.

First, no worthwhile question of being can expect quick answers. The existence of things is "strange" and "disguised" – not simply **given** to an observer, nor given all at once. What **is** might be disclosed, but also perhaps not. That there might be some kind of "mystery" of being has alarmed many philosophers.

In Rilke's words, ... *the strange disguised phenomenon ... possible situations which might disclose its nature.*

Second, the meditative state with its possible disclosures can be lost, covered over by the call of the "everyday world"; of labouring to deal with the demands or largesses of the tourist-poet and of others.

... the immediate loss of the thoughtful expression, the momentary confusion, the reversion to the ... usual silly baksheesh face ...

Questions of being can be **evaded**. We can simply accept that things "exist", and turn away from questioning, towards **practical everyday** matters...

And thirdly, who is concerned with all this? Certainly the poet.

For Rilke, being is a proper concern of poets. It is poets who should speak it, and speak our awarenesses of it.

A questioning of being might need "poetic" language...

That too has alarmed philosophers. Is this the end of all logic, all reason, all truth and all proofs, all systematized argument?

And this again suggests a possible evasion.

We could throw any question of being over to **logical reasoning**, or to **scientific method**: e.g. to the accumulation of "facts" about the world; absorbing ourselves in descriptions of what things are like - not **that** they are...

19

Natural Attitudes

So is Rilke, and Heidegger too, pursuing some beguiling question conjured in the artifice of philosophy? Isn't "being" so dramatically easy to grasp that it needs no lavish care from poets and philosophers?

For instance: how do we know that things exist? We can see them, or hear them, or feel them, etc. **Sensory perception** offers the route and the answer. Rilke and his rower are out after some purely phantasmal realm, inherently untestable, unprovable and perhaps nonsensical.

This attitude has its counterpart in philosophy. For instance, in **Empiricism**.

Empiricists hold that knowledge must be derived from experience of the world and that the "direct" experience of sensory perceptions is vital.
Observation and experiment will rule.

Positivism *pushes the case further. Philosophy should proceed like the* ***sciences...***

From such perspectives, there can scarcely be a *question* of being. It is a basic pre-supposition, what one *assumes* before anything else.

Beings and Being

Heidegger had a deep suspicion of all empiricist and positivist philosophies, and all scientific thought of the usual kind. If to think and speak of being demands attunement to mystery and poetic language – then, so be it. Call it a day for empiricist philosophy and science ...

Heidegger articulated this in a crucially important distinction:
BEINGS and **BEING**.

BEINGS (*Seiendes*, or singular *das Seiende*) are **entities**, having characteristics that define or determine them.

They are "that which is" – perhaps "things" in the world, perhaps events, relations or processes... And they can be studied as the objects of science and everyday knowledge...

BEING (*Sein*) denotes the **being of** these entities, being as such: the fact that they have their existence, that they **are**.

This is the proper concern of philosophy.

And to point up Heidegger's distinctions, some English translations use a capital: beings and **B**eing ...

So Heidegger distinguishes between ...

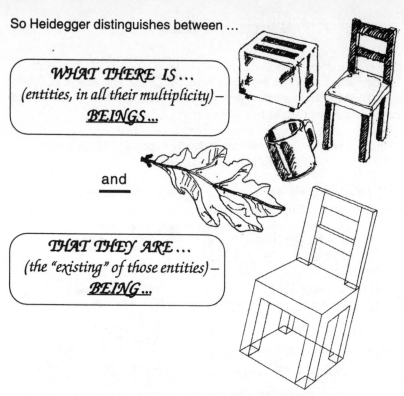

> ***WHAT THERE IS ...***
> *(entities, in all their multiplicity) –*
> ***BEINGS ...***

and

> ***THAT THEY ARE ...***
> *(the "existing" of those entities) –*
> ***BEING ...***

And two kinds of statement can be made.

ONTIC: a statement ***about*** some entity or other ...

ONTOLOGICAL: a statement concerning the ***being*** of such entities...

Heidegger took ***being*** as such, and ***ontological*** statements about it, as his proper province. In his view, the sciences and much Western philosophy tried to amass "knowledge of particular entities, their characteristics, their relations to each other", etc...

But this preoccupation with ***beings***, and with ***ontic*** knowledge, leads to a forgetting of being.

The major difficulty: being is not *a* being. It is not an entity. Nor is it a class or category of entities – nor some property or characteristic of them.

Being and beings are **different**. Heidegger calls this an "ontological difference"...

> *So being is not any "thing".*
> *It is not simply available to the senses.*
> *You can't just go and have a look at it, nor listen*
> *in on it, to find out how it's doing...*

> *...You can't transport it, <u>nor, crucially, sell it</u> ...*
> *– how could we know how much we were getting?*

Resisting sensory apprehension, characterization, disposability, commodification, measurement, etc., being is highly resistant to our usual ways of dealing with, and thinking about, beings ...

That is why Rilke thought his boatman had a problem.

Obedient Piety: Beginnings in Theology

Heidegger's first formulation of the "question of being" did not arrive quickly. It took some ten years' reading in philosophy and other fields. Ontology – thinking about being – has been part of Western philosophy since its inauguration in Greece in the 5th century BC.

It was a long reading list...

...But I entered university to study THEOLOGY...

It was a trajectory with familial foundations...

He was born into a pious, petty-bourgeois Catholic family in Messkirch, Baden-Württemburg, where his father was the sexton of St Martin's church. These were the heartlands of the ancient Swabian region of Southern Germany, conservative and conserving; rooted in a rural agrarian economy, dependent on static social hierarchies and long-established systems of land ownership, labour, religious lore and customs.

Heidegger was destined for the priesthood.

He trained at the Freiburg Jesuit Seminary alongside his high school and university education. In 1909 a church scholarship paid for his entry to Freiburg University.

Freiburg connected to a different world, one marked by **modernity**: burgeoning metropolitan cities, time-compressing transport and tele-communications (the telephone, for commerce of all kinds), industrialization, mechanization (new labour patterns, new forms of social life).

A world of new invention, permeated by the rhetorics of modernism: progress, change, valorization of the new.

Though small and rural-provincial, Freiburg was situated in a network of respected European universities (Vienna, Heidelberg, Marburg, Göttingen, Strasbourg, Zurich). They took "new ideas" to lie in their jurisdiction.

Heidegger entered a world of fitful collisions between continuity and change, settled existences and dynamic mobilities.

Pious Disobedience

Heidegger's first studies were theological: Old and New Testament Scriptures, messianic prophesy, theory of revelation, moral theology, canonic law, theological cosmology, etc. But in 1911 he abandoned his training for the priesthood, and turned his university studies first towards mathematics, and then philosophy: its history and its specialized fields – epistemology, metaphysics, logic, ethics, and so on. Nevertheless ...

Without the theological origin I would never have come upon the path of thinking.

Meanings of "Being"

Across these studies, Heidegger restlessly pursued a problem: the term "being" had **meant** many different things to those who used it. Out of this was later to arise his first formulation of the being-question: what was the **meaning** of being?

A mid-18th century convention offered a structure...

Philosophy had three major epochs: those of the ancient GREEKS, the MEDIEVAL SCHOLASTICS, and MODERN PHILOSOPHY. Heidegger worked on all three, reading each in the light of the others.

First, the Greeks.

*For Plato (427-347 BC), every being had an **ideal** existence, as a perfect, unchanging "form"...*

What we experience as visible, audible, tactile beings are merely imperfect reflections or "copies" of the ideal beings.

To Heidegger, and many others, **Aristotle** (384-322 BC) was a more useful figure.

Aristotle made many contributions to ontology, and among them, a "theory of categories", highly influential on Medieval thought and resonant even into the modern age.

The Rule of Substance

For Aristotle, the realm of being would be divided into different types, or categories, of beings...

In the first place, beings come either as *SUBSTANCES* or as *ATTRIBUTES*.

A SUBSTANCE is what something is in itself, identifiable and separable from other substances: e.g., animals and plants, stars and planets, and also artefacts like tables and chairs, tools, etc.

If we ask, "What is it?", we can say it is a ***this*** or a ***that*** – for instance, it is a rat or a star, a philosopher or an umbrella.

All other categories are ATTRIBUTES of these substances. An attribute is some kind of quality or characteristic that substances have – e.g. a substance might be purple, or pliable, poisonous or permeable.

So we could inquire of an umbrella's attributes ...

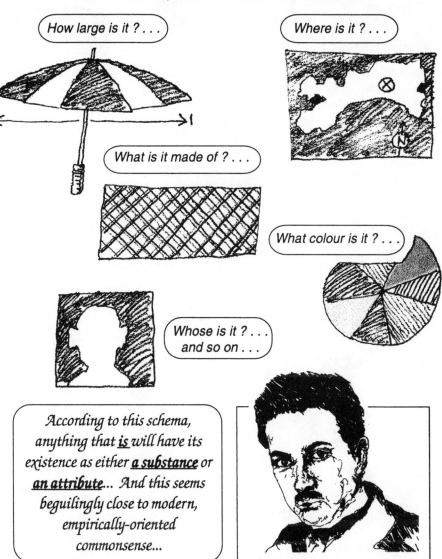

How large is it ? ...

Where is it ? ...

What is it made of ? ...

What colour is it ? ...

Whose is it ? ...
and so on ...

According to this schema, anything that __is__ will have its existence as either __a substance__ or __an attribute__... And this seems beguilingly close to modern, empirically-oriented commonsense...

But another statement is possible: ***"The umbrella is."***
We announce that it exists, that it has its being. And its ***being*** is neither a substance ***nor*** an attribute. That was Heidegger's problem.

Aristotle had categorized beings, but offered no satisfactory account of being. Each of the categories marks out *a type of being*, and how it can be known – but there was no single, unified concept of being as such...

Aristotle, aware of the problem, tried many solutions – but notions of **substance** remained for him the basis of being. This became one of the principal strands of Western **ontology**. Notions of "substance", however, had problems...

Could they hold satisfactorily for, say, mathematical or logical entities? "3" might exist, but as a mathematical concept, and not in the same way that an umbrella exists as a material tool. Likewise, "sadness", "elation" or other psychic states exist, but deflect no rain...

... And theological entities resist description in terms of substance ...

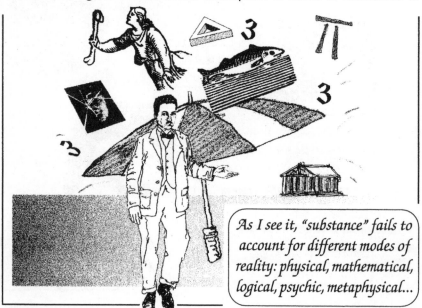

As I see it, "substance" fails to account for different modes of reality: physical, mathematical, logical, psychic, metaphysical...

Against the tyranny of substance, Heidegger read Aristotle's ontology **through** its Medieval Christian reception...

Scholasticism

From about 800 AD, Christian theologians had begun to exploit Greek philosophy. Would philosophy win out over theology? Or was some synthesis possible – as suggested by 13th century Scholastic thinkers **St Thomas Aquinas** (1225-74) and **John Duns Scotus** (1266-1308)? Both tried to read Aristotle in ways that conformed with Christian theology.

Heidegger in 1915 wrote a Dissertation on a text supposedly by Duns Scotus, Scottish Franciscan and teacher at Oxford and Paris. How did the Scholastics negotiate "being"?

*Duns Scotus retained Aristotle's ontology but subtly shifted its emphasis. What was important was HOW the various entities are known: how they are **thought** to exist.*

That was important for Heidegger. But like other Scholastics, Duns saw that Aristotle's ontology had no place for God, an important being for Christian theologians. As a transcendental Being, the uncaused causer, God had to encompass and generate all other beings – all substances and attributes.

So God's being could not be simply tacked on to Aristotle's list as just one more being among others. Effectively, "God" – not "substance" – now became the ground of being, its ultimate origin and its explanation.

Modern Philosophy

Heidegger later came to think that any attempt to find a "ground" for being – e.g. in substance, or some transcendental super-Being – was an *evasion* of the question of being. Such strategies were all "onto-theologies": they diverted our understanding of being, by trying to explain it as grounded in something else.

Were there other possibilities? Not content with the Greeks and the Scholastics, Heidegger was reading extensively into MODERN philosophy.

The crucial development has been "Cartesian rationalism".

I think therefore I am.

René Descartes (1596-1650) had proposed a distinction between SUBJECT and OBJECT: the "knowing subject" was identified with the conscious, rational mind – the Ego – whose own processes of reasoning offered the assured knowledge of the "objects" of the world, "out there" beyond it.

The Legacy of Descartes

Philosophy was offered some new directions. It had to explicate this mind, its modes of reasoning, and its relations to its objects – the things "out there" which it reasoned *about*.

The subject-object distinction, and the stress on rational consciousness, became powerful tools for the philosophy of the 18th century Enlightenment.

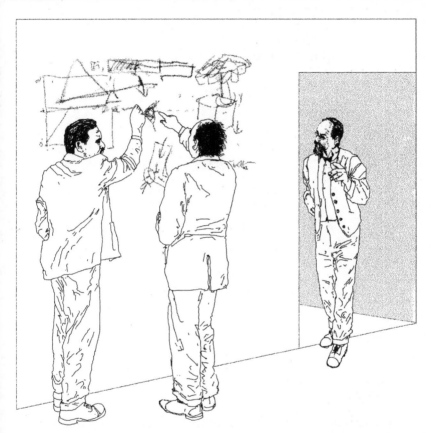

The Cartesian tradition had a later, radical reformer: **Edmund Husserl** (1859-1938), mathematician, logician and founder of modern PHENOMENOLOGY.

Heidegger was caught up in Husserl's work from his earliest student days, and the ties were deep.

Phenomenology

"Both volumes of the 1901 *Logical Investigations* lay on my desk in the theology seminary ever since my first semester there. I remained so fascinated by it that I read it again and again in the years to follow. The spell extended to the appearance of the sentence structure and the title page ..."

It was more than a hypnotizing talisman.

In 1916, Husserl arrived in Freiburg as Professor of Philosophy, and from 1919 to 1923 Heidegger was employed as his assistant. What was so attractive about phenomenology?

*Deeply set against empiricism and the positivist sciences, Husserl proposed a study of **consciousness** — not of any psychological particulars, gathered experimentally, but of what might be **universally true** of the human mind.*

The First World War

Universal truths of the mind, 1914-18 ?

In those years, more than 15 million men of the major nation-states massacred each other in the interests of their respective capitalisms. Lenin established the world's first Communist state, and in Germany in 1918, the ruling dynasty was overthrown and revolutionary soviets temporarily established.

Heidegger's deepening encounter with phenomenology came at this time. Yet he remained virtually silent on all these events.

His first three stints of military service, amounting to ten weeks in 1914-15, were interrupted by ill-health. His four months against American troops at the Western Front, from September 1918, came when the Armistice was under negotiation.

Meanwhile, he finished his thesis, taught Catholic philosophy from 1915, met his future wife Elfriede Petri (summer 1916), and they married in 1917. He opened personal contacts with Husserl in 1917, and dealt with a crisis of faith – Elfriede was Lutheran. Heidegger renounced Catholicism in January 1919.

Did the war affect Heidegger's work? His silence could suggest unconcern, repression or displacement, or a refusal to take world events as important. But his later texts carry some hints – a sense of fundamental crisis, of anarchistic individualism as the only way that humans can transcend the situations into which they are thrown.

And a darker hint is his known admiration for the totalitarian social doctrines of the novelist **Ernst Jünger** (b. 1895), an acquaintance and correspondent.

Did this extend to *The Storm of Steel* and *Fire and Blood*, in which Jünger turned his war experiences into a conservative-anarchist mythology of heroized masculinity and exalted violence?

We cannot be sure. But Heidegger's preoccupation was the very different world of **phenomenology** and Husserl's detailed, logical and painstaking search for "pure consciousness".

Towards Pure Consciousness

Phenomenology has some peculiar features, with ontological implications (Husserl called it a "philosophy of Absolute Being"). To follow Husserl's manoeuvres is also to track Heidegger's early trajectories.

> *How does Husserl locate his "universally-true" consciousness?*

> By phenomenological REDUCTION. Suspend any attention to mere particulars, "bracket" them out ... Remove them from the scene, and what is left will be the essential, universal structures of the mind.

REDUCTION ONE:

The first thing to go is reality. Husserl is emphatic: it does of course exist. But real objects are not objects *in consciousness*. Their study can be safely left to the positive sciences.
They are of no concern to the proper phenomenologist.

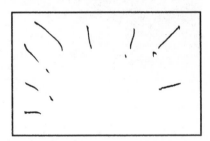

It's a surprising move. The implications become clearer if we follow a second "bracketing"...

REDUCTION TWO: Isolate the *objects* and the *acts* of consciousness.

OBJECTS appear in consciousness. To appear in our minds at all, some kind of mental activity, or ACT, must be performed. That too must be studied.

For example, "a white book on a blue table" can be conjured up, or constituted, in our minds. So can "the causes of the First World War"...

...These are OBJECTS appearing in consciousness (even though we use exactly the same **phrases** to designate their real counterparts)...

Husserl calls them "noemata".

However, the ACTS of consciousness which conjured them are not white, nor on any table, and don't cause a war that has already happened.

Acts of consciousness include analyzing, judging, reflecting, adjudicating, calculating, etc.; but also imagining, willing, remembering, expecting, hoping, etc. (Husserl's term: "noeses".)

Objects in Consciousness

Crucially, the object need have no actual, real existence. As an object in consciousness, "a centaur" has a similar status to "the Prime Minister of Britain". They lie in the same realm.

*So it is not the business of the phenomenologist to check whether anything in the real world **corresponds** to what turns up in consciousness...*

The task is to analyze what turns up... and how...

Even a real Prime Minister can appear in consciousness characterized as a "fiction" or a "recollection"... or indeed as a "corporeal reality".
It depends whether the **act** of consciousness was one of imaginative fancy, or memory – or some kind of judgement, expectation or calculation of "realness".

Solipsism

Can a "sensory perception" offer assured knowledge of reality, of what exists? It could be illusory, hallucinatory or otherwise deceptive (sticks "bend" in water, without bending).

*The experience in consciousness of **having** a perception is the only phenomenological certainty.*

Where does this lead?

Conscious acts and objects are the only entities of which an assured, foundational knowledge is possible. (As critics quickly noted, Husserl leans towards SOLIPSISM: the only properly or ultimately knowable world is that constituted in one's own consciousness.)

But what are the implications for ontology?

A third, final reduction is needed …

The Transcendental Ego

REDUCTION THREE: Objects and acts are of many different types –
they come *plural*.

Was there some single unifying realm for all of them, something that could
be claimed as their ultimate basis or foundation? Husserl thought there **had**
to be. **Consciousness itself** ...

Consciousness itself is not given to awareness – we cannot know it directly
(only its objects and acts). But for Husserl it is a logical necessity.

Something has to be the
site of relation of all the
different acts and objects.

*Husserl, echoing Descartes,
called it the "Transcendental Ego".*

How is it reached?
Bracket out even the objects and acts. The Transcendental Ego is what
remains. And Husserl equates it with *Absolute Being* ...

Husserl's claim is connected to the "bracketing" of reality:

"Phenomenology does not deny the existence of the real world. Its sole task is to clarify the *meaning* of this world – the *sense in which everyone accepts it,* rightly, as really existing."

The real world exists, but it needs the **Transcendental Ego** to conjure it up as such, to produce the *sense* that "it exists". That Ego is then the ground of the meaning of being, the only site in which such meaning can fundamentally arise. And in itself, it is Absolute Being.

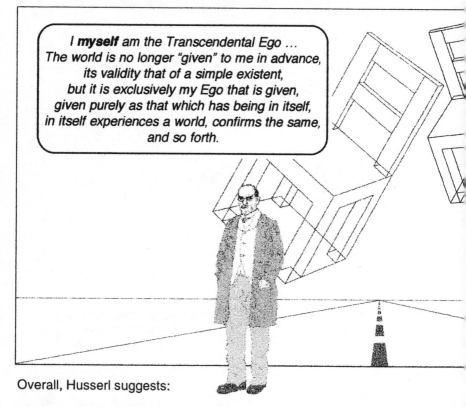

I *myself* am the Transcendental Ego …
The world is no longer "given" to me in advance,
its validity that of a simple existent,
but it is exclusively my Ego that is given,
given purely as that which has being in itself,
in itself experiences a world, confirms the same,
and so forth.

Overall, Husserl suggests:

● Consciousness brings *its own* objects into being (though it falls short at bringing *reality* into being).

● HOW we become aware of things, in consciousness, is crucial to our sense of what IS.

● The ultimate "IS": the Ego, as pure consciousness.

Heidegger and Phenomenology

So ultimately, how did Husserl construe being ? Not as "substance", not as "God" but as "absolute consciousness"...

... And Heidegger?

I was deeply impressed by Husserl's central notion – entities "appear in consciousness"...

That is how they are known – how we become aware of them.

But Heidegger began to have doubts about this abstract, sovereign "consciousness". Did it rule unchallenged? Entities might turn up ... but did they turn up *only* for a purified, disembodied Ego?

And strangely, the doubts were first expressed by Husserl himself.

Limits of Phenomenology

To Husserl, a dangerous chasm seemed to open up between *theoretical* modes of consciousness, and those of ordinary everyday life.

Husserl in 1913:
"I am in the world, it is continually 'present' for me: a world of facts, values and goods, a PRACTICAL world. Things stand there as objects to be used, the 'table' with its 'books', the 'glass to drink from', the 'vase', the 'piano' and so forth. It is to *this* world that I bring my comparing, counting, presupposing, inferring – the theorizing activity of consciousness."

And there is more …

The Practical World

Unlike most philosophers, Husserl noticed the PRACTICAL, lived-in world, **and** the STATES OF MIND, perhaps emotional, in which we live in it.

*I can be in an "arithmetic" world, as long as I adopt the arithmetic standpoint; but the ordinary, natural world is **always** there for me.*

If the ordinary practical world is there, always, it comes first. It has to be there for someone before they can launch into abstract calculations, theorizing about Transcendental Egos, etc.

Perhaps, then, an ontologist should pay attention to it.

Husserl, having noticed it, kept putting it back in brackets. But Heidegger set off on a dramatically new path – towards **being** as it was encountered and made meaningful, in PRACTICAL EVERYDAY LIFE.

And curiously, the path cycled right back to Aristotle.

Aristotle's *Phronesis*

Heidegger's return was not to the Aristotle of the "categories" of beings. In the *Nichomachean Ethics*, Aristotle set out PRACTICAL modes by which the world is known, for example, ***phronesis.***

This is having an eye out for how things are done, and why, and having a readiness to deal with the world... to make decisions in it.

As a way of encountering what exists, this is different to "categorizing" it...

...I set the practical Aristotle against the categorizing Aristotle.

Heidegger's "Destruction"

What was going on? Traditional interpretations of Aristotle (by the Medieval Scholastics and their late-19th century revivalists) had stressed the categories. For Heidegger, these interpretations had to be "destroyed".

In their place, a new reading of Aristotle would be offered: an Aristotle who encountered being practically.

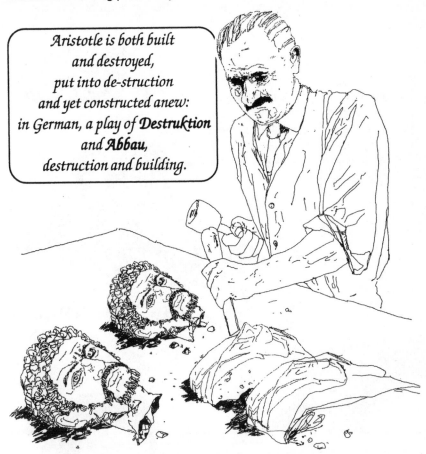

*Aristotle is both built and destroyed, put into de-struction and yet constructed anew: in German, a play of **Destruktion** and **Abbau**, destruction and building.*

This strange double movement became one of Heidegger's familiar tactics. And it has had a celebrated after-life, as the kind of manoeuvre for which Jacques Derrida in the 1960s adopted the term, *deconstruction*.

But Aristotle was not Heidegger's only resource.

Factical Life

Heidegger had been reading **Wilhelm Dilthey** (1833-1911), philosopher of history, early contributor to the human and social sciences, and a critic of Husserl. Dilthey emphasized "factical life" – the lived experience of the practical and social worlds, with all the perceptions, evaluations and responses that that implies. Knowledge of this "factical life" can only be *interpretative*. To Dilthey, a person was *not* some isolated, solipsistic Ego, having its fundamental existence as an abstracted, purified consciousness.

> People live socially, always with others, and they live historically – their experiences of the world change in time.

> I became convinced that "factical life" did indeed come first – **that** is where entities make their appearance, in the first instance, **before** they become objects of theoretical knowledge.

"Destroyed" Greek philosophy, deep theological readings, and modern philosophy – out of this volatile cocktail, a declaration against Husserl, at the very root.

The Transcendental Ego is a fantastic fiction.
We need to get at the totality of the subject which *experiences* *the world*
and not to some BLOODLESS THINKING THING
which merely theoretically *thinks* *the world.*

Phenomenology was to be treated to a new beginning.

The Hermeneutics of Facticity

Escaping Husserl's employment to become Associate Professor at Marbach in 1923, Heidegger worked out the project: An Interpretative Analysis of Factual Life, or as he called it, a "hermeneutics of facticity". (*Hermeneutics*, from the Greek "interpretation", as later applied to Scripture.)

How could he proceed? Turn towards empiricism or some kind of materialism? That would bind him into ONTIC knowledges, turning him away from the properly ONTOLOGICAL question of being.

But Heidegger insisted that being is always the being *of* something.

So, to study it, select a something and analyze it. Which something? One entity suggested itself: the __human__ entity.

Dasein

In his 1924 lecture, *The Concept of Time*, Heidegger proposed nothing less than a reconceptualization of what it is to be human. "Our inquiry points in the direction of DASEIN …" But what did Heidegger mean by "Dasein"?

Dasein … *that entity in its being which we know as human life; this entity in the specificity of its being, the entity that we each ourselves are, which each of us finds in the fundamental assertion:*
I am.

So "Dasein" seems to overlap with what is normally called a "human being".

However, *Dasein* literally means "there-being", from *Da* (there) and *Sein* (being). For Heidegger, it denoted the human entity in all its **ways of being.**

"Dasein" was an 18th century translation of the Latin **praesentia**, generally meaning "existence". Kant and Husserl both used it.

"Dasein" can't be reduced to notions of biological bodies or a zoological species, nor to minds or consciousnesses...

...nor any other preconceptions gathered around words like "man", "humanity", "subject", "subjectivity", "person", etc.

Heidegger's term was almost a blank space.

His initial task: a comprehensive analysis of *Dasein* in its "ordinary average everydayness".

Next step: relate *Dasein* to **time**. After that: analysis of being "in general".

His book, *Being and Time*, is the compendium of his thoughts on human modes of being, and on time, up to 1927.

Being and Time

Heidegger needed a publication to support his application for the Chair of Philosophy at Freiburg, recently vacated by Husserl. *Being and Time*, hastily published, has been named his "major work" and granted high status.

Some have seen it as a text central to European philosophy, and perhaps the most celebrated philosophical work of the 20th century.

But few introductions proceed without health warnings.

It is a complex and densely argued text, often using a strange, resonant but esoteric vocabulary, difficult in German and highly resistant to translation. And across its 500 pages, Heidegger sets out many innovative concepts.

These were to have powerful repercussions in contemporary thought.

The Analysis of Dasein

Measured one way or another, *Being and Time* is unfinished. It deals only with *Dasein* and its being in time – not the central ontological question: **being as such**. Heidegger had not, however, forgotten his question.

Do we in our time have an answer to the question of what we really mean by the word "being"?
<u>*Not at all...*</u>
But are we nowadays even perplexed at our inability to understand the expression "being"?
<u>*Not at all...*</u>

*... So our aim in the following treatise is to work out the question of the meaning of **being** and to do so concretely.*

How is this to be a "concrete" analysis? By starting with *Dasein* as BEING-IN-THE-WORLD and BEING-WITH-OTHERS.

Let's start with the first ...

1. Being-in-the-World

Dasein's being-IN-the world involves relations to other entities. Heidegger makes a distinction: the READY-TO-HAND and the PRESENT-AT-HAND.

Things which are **READY-TO-HAND** *(zuhanden)* are available for practical use; they are handy, utilitarian, instrumental.

Heidegger's example: a hammer.

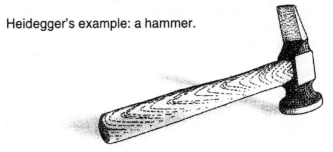

It is a simple thing in the world, a tool. Primarily and usually, in everyday living, it is grasped in its utility, its fitness or not for a particular task.

But the hammer is not ***entirely*** simple.

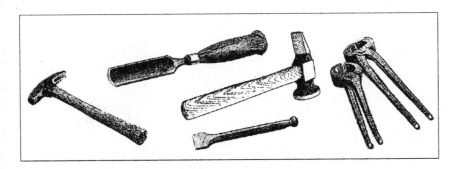

Dasein understands it within a NETWORK of other entities: related tools, raw materials, the task it is used for, its end result or product, etc.
In this network, the hammer is understood to have its existence *as* something ready-to-hand.

Dasein fundamentally *is* in its relations to ready-to-hand entities. Heidegger names these: relations of CONCERN.

Presence-at-Hand

The **PRESENT-AT-HAND** *(vorhanden)* is encountered in a mode of detached contemplation or observation, not of immediate utility. This is the preferred mode of the specialized intellectual disciplines of philosophy and the sciences.

In particular ("ontic") cases, some passage is possible.

*The "south wind" can be **present-at-hand**, something to contemplate, perhaps in theoretical science...*

...But it can also be put to use — for instance, to generate power.

Heidegger has a suspicion against treating things as present-at-hand. It is ONE way of encountering entities – but not the only, the first, or the most usual way.

It isolates entities, separating them from their networks and distancing them from *Dasein*, shading out *Dasein's* fundamentally "concernful" relations with them.

Understanding

For Heidegger the practical, ready-to-hand has primacy. Hence, his term UNDERSTANDING, but used in a strange way to mean the awareness of entities that arrives in the closest kinds of practical use, handling, and so on.

> *Understanding is not intellectual, not theoretical, and it might not even be articulated. But it is Dasein's first and fundamental way of **being-IN-the-world**.*

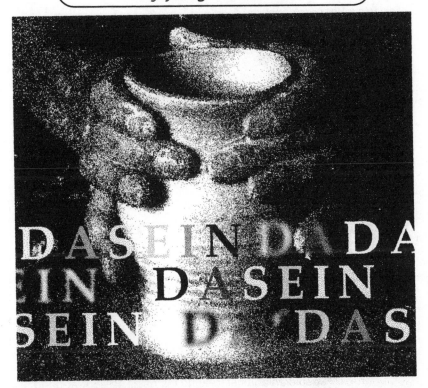

If practical understanding comes first, it comes *before* science or philosophy. These are special, modified cases of it.

And what they have taken as ontologically fundamental (e.g. conceptualized "substance", "God", "consciousness" etc.) is **not** fundamental to Heidegger's ontology.

States of Mind

Along with understanding, *Dasein's* being-in-the-world involves STATES OF MIND: affects (emotions), but also more broadly, moods, or **dispositions.**

Husserl had hinted at this. Heidegger provided the analysis (for example, of "fear") and claimed "dispositions" as fundamental to *Dasein's* being. It adds another strand to his critique of philosophy.

Are these "states of mind" proper objects of study?

Are they open to rational, logical methods and procedures?

Can they be treated as "objects", available for measurement, locatable in proper places?

Resistant to these approaches, they are nevertheless part of Dasein's being-in-the-world, and ontologically fundamental.

Where does this leave philosophy?

Heidegger has used the question of being to question philosophy ...

Descartes' Amnesia

Philosophers and scientists have **forgotten** that practical "understanding" and "states of mind" are fundamental.

Galileo forgets his own being-in-the-world, and so do Newton, Kant, Hegel, et al. The concept of being-in-the-world goes especially counter to Cartesian modes of thought.

> *In Descartes' subject-object distinction,*
> *the "object" is taken to be something*
> *<u>external</u> to the mind of the knowing subject.*

> It is "out there".
> And the "subject" becomes simply
> the conscious, rational mind,
> "given" before its relation to the object.

Heidegger disrupts this.

IN-the-World ...

Against Descartes, and all derived or revised Cartesianisms, Heidegger argues that ...

● *Dasein* is already IN-the-world.

Human life is not some "subject" that has to perform some trick in order to enter the world.

Dasein needs no "trick" − no formulae from science, no gambits from philosophy. It *is* that way.

● *Dasein* is not primarily a detached observer of "objects", but a "concerned" user of practical entities. "*Dasein* deals with the world, in the manner of performing, effecting and completing."

So the world is not something "out there", external − but **part of** *Dasein's* being, as being-in.

Heidegger can make this strange case because *Dasein* is not reducible to a "physical body", a separated "mind", etc.

... and IN-ness

In Heidegger's hands, Cartesian thought suffers other deformations. For instance, something strange happens to SPACE.

When Heidegger writes of being-in-the-world, "in-ness" means: bound up in relations of practical concern, and states of mind. This is not being "in" a geometrically-understood *space.* The world is more a workshop of *Dasein's* making than a scientifically measurable calculable space.

So practical concern comes *before* geometrical science.

In my model, space is a "pure extension" of linear directions, measurable and calculable, and "substances" are extensions within that space.

But from a practical point of view __a place__ is not merely a point in a set of fixed, abstract, grid-like co-ordinates.

A place is part of a system of *practical engagements*, of concern. And this leads to some strange, but very ordinary, phenomena.

The World's Places

For instance, in practical concern, **distance** becomes de-geometricized. It "bends" into some strange shapes. A caller on a telephone is nearer than a person in the next room, if our attention – our concern, our understanding, our disposition in our being as *Dasein* – is with the call and not the neighbour.

Practical concern, understanding and states of mind – __before__ geometry and other rationalizings – can make space stretch or contract.

Mathematically calculable space is annulled. For *Dasein* as being-IN, things are brought nearer, sent further off, in ways that confound the purity of measurement.

2. Being-with-Others

Dasein is not in-the-world in some regally isolated, solipsistic state. Heidegger recognized Husserl's problem, and answered it with a surprising logic. *Dasein* has its being as BEING-WITH-OTHERS – but in problematic ways.

First, each *Dasein* is indeed UNIQUE. "*Dasein* determines itself as 'I am'. It is in each case its own and is specific as its own."

But can it always know this, and live it fully? Its condition is difficult …

*It is not I myself who for the **most** part and **on average** am my Dasein, but the Others.*

No one is himself in everydayness.

No one is himself in everydayness.

Dasein is subject to take-over bids by the Others. It exists as an "I am" but also as an "I-am-with-the-Others".

It cannot be entirely or securely an "I am", if it also has to be a "with-them".

Them

Or as Heidegger puts it:

> "... in the practical public environment, in utilizing public means of transport and in making use of information services such as the newspaper, every Other is like the next. One's own *Dasein* dissolves completely into the kind of being of 'the Others' ..."

Dasein loses itself in others.

Who does this? No one in particular.

The "who" is *das Man*, in German an impersonal pronoun. The nearest English equivalent is perhaps "one" ("One would say that, wouldn't one?").

Das Man is also translated as "the Them" or "the They" with senses of "People" or "the Public", taken as an impersonal, faceless collectivity.

The Dictatorship of the Others

When in everyday living *Dasein* dissolves itself in Others, it becomes the Others. So the Others as Others dissolve too: they are now part of *Dasein*.

As such, the They is very hard to identify. In this lies its power.

"In its inconspicuousness and unascertainability, the real dictatorship of the They is unfolded. We take pleasure and enjoy ourselves as *they* take pleasure; we read, see and judge about literature and art as *they* see and judge; we find shocking what *they* find shocking. The 'they', which all are, prescribes the kind of being of everydayness."

Mass Society

What was Heidegger up to? Fundamental ontology, or commentary on the condition of *contemporary society*?

He offers an unusual philosophical response to "mass society" theories, propagated by sociologists **Max Weber** (1864-1920) and **Emile Durkheim** (1859-1917), analyzed by Frankfurt School Marxists like **T.W. Adorno** (1903-69) and many others.

These theories influenced philosophy. For instance, Heidegger knew well the work of **Karl Jaspers** (1883-1969), Heidelberg "philosopher of existence". Jaspers' influential *Man in the Modern Age*, conceives a struggle between a "life of the spirit" and the "enslaving forces" of machine-age modern civilization.

It is one of the most familiar and powerful oppositions of the 20th century.

The "enslaving forces" were those of modernity and its culture: the intense mechanization of industrial labour, the standardization of products; the cities; the new culture – commercialized entertainment, "massed" sporting events, cinema, radio – the popular journalism, the manufacture of "public opinion"...

Industrial Misery, Commercial Happiness

Out of this came the "mass-effect": a culture of mindless uniformity and deadly conformity, crushing the possibilities for "independent decision", vaporizing "freedom of action".

The particulars varied, but the vision was widely recognizable: modern society produced a terrifying obliteration of "the individual". To Jaspers in 1932, no science or positivistic philosophy could help.

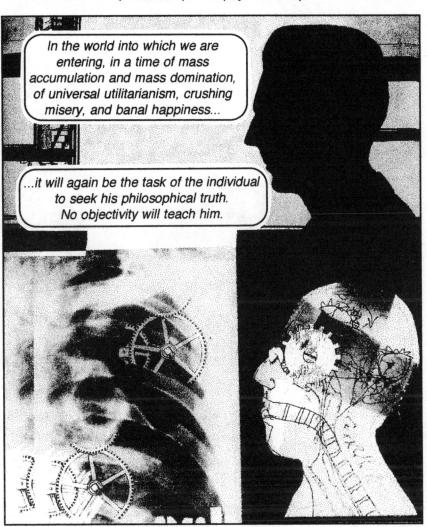

Pop Culture and They

Such theories of "mass culture" can be read as the horrified reaction of an élite, conservative intelligentsia to the challenges of "pop culture" and capitalist commodification.

> *All these fads – jazz, Charlie Chaplin, Plato in paperback – a disaster!*

But some of Heidegger's Marxist contemporaries, like **Bertolt Brecht** (1898-1956), thought otherwise ...

> *Popular culture can be a vital resource of revolutionary politics.*

But Heidegger shared in the negative vision.

His They is not *simply* "the mass"; nor is *Dasein* "the individual". But the rhetorical pattern is the same: absorption of unique ("my own") *Dasein* into the They, is a debilitating condition.
Heidegger's measured philosophical sentences carry an edge of hysterical denial ("*That* cannot be me!").

But what precisely was so threatening about *das Man*? Heidegger lays out the case.

Publicness (*Offentlichkeit*): identification with the faceless "public" is a letting-go of one's being.

"Thus the particular *Dasein* in its everydayness is **disburdened** by the They."

Averageness, mediocrity (*Durchschnittlichkeit*): Heidegger rails against "levelling down".

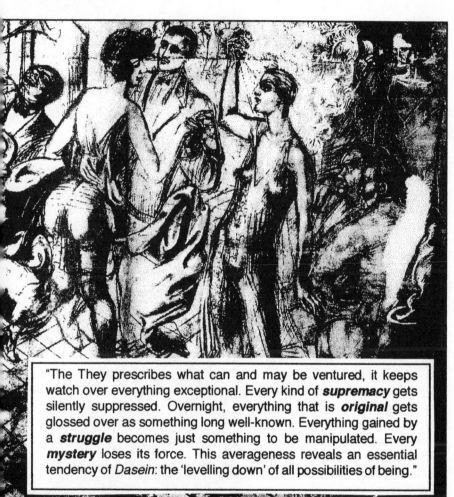

"The They prescribes what can and may be ventured, it keeps watch over everything exceptional. Every kind of **supremacy** gets silently suppressed. Overnight, everything that is **original** gets glossed over as something long well-known. Everything gained by a **struggle** becomes just something to be manipulated. Every **mystery** loses its force. This averageness reveals an essential tendency of *Dasein*: the 'levelling down' of all possibilities of being."

The vocabulary is Nietzschean: struggle and effort towards supremacy, active unbound forces of origination against those of "mediocrity". The list goes on ...

Averageness

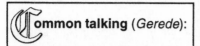 **ommon talking** (*Gerede*):

The everyday speaking of the public world, a speaking of "average understandability", perhaps "chattering".

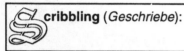 **cribbling** (*Geschriebe*):

Its counterpart in writing – popular writing, commonly intelligible, in newspapers and popular fiction; writing that people want and expect to read; absorbing, distracting, "disburdening" writing.

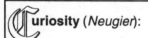 **uriosity** (*Neugier*):

A positive attitude? For Heidegger, curiosity is a desire for new fashions (what *das Man* is up to) and for vicarious experiences. Like common talk and scribbling, it infects philosophy too.

In pursuit of the meaning of being, Heidegger is not a champion of "popular culture".

Fallenness

Dasein's everyday condition is FALLENNESS: absorption IN the world and WITH the Them; all-embracing preoccupation with the ready-to-hand, under the sway of the Them.

Made over into philosophy, "fallenness" still resonates theologically. *Dasein* is fallen like sinful man before God. And what does Fallenness comprise?

Temptation:

The invitation to be absorbed in the world and to surrender to the Them.

Contentment:

Dasein's "restlessness" is washed away in the satisfactions of the everyday world; a self-manufactured, secular ablution of *Dasein's* complex being.

And borrowed from the Danish philosopher **Søren Kierkegaard** (1813-55) and others –

Alienation:

Cutting oneself off from the (ontologically) true, unified self.

Falling is a basic kind of being for *Dasein*.

Thrownness and Projective Possibility

Is this everyday world avoidable? *Dasein* is THROWN into it. Thrownness is being in a world which is outside *Dasein's* control – like saying "to be thrown into despair". The state is not **chosen**. The world contains things for which *Dasein* is not responsible and did not choose.

And yet, Dasein still has room for manoeuvre, choices, responsibility.

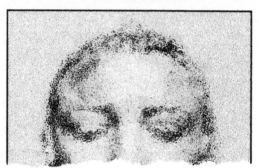

PROJECTION is *Dasein's* projection forwards onto this or that POSSIBILITY for itself. What or who could it possibly be? Potentiality is part of its being.

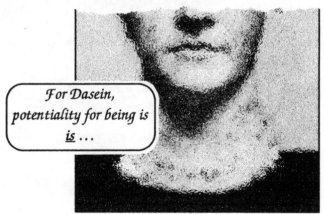

For Dasein, potentiality for being is is ...

But thrownness entangles possibilities. *Dasein* cannot just project onto anything (without risking total loss of itself). Restraints include the contexts of projection, *Dasein's* limited skills, knowledges, etc.

So *Dasein* has its being in a strained, ambiguous struggle between thrownness and possibility. *Dasein* is "**thrown possibility**, through and through".

Care

Being IN and being WITH, negotiating the ready-to-hand and the present-at-hand, the They-world and fallenness, thrownness and projected possibilities, *Dasein* scarcely seems **unified**.

Yet Heidegger insists on its unity, and he proposes a unifying concept: CARE.

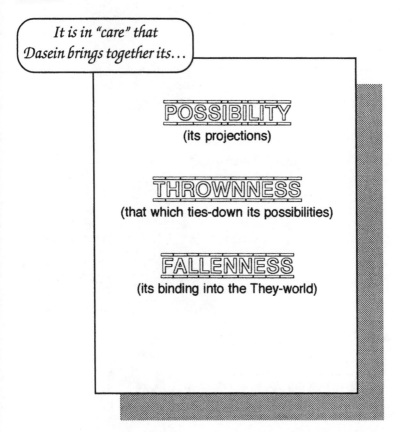

It is in "care" that Dasein brings together its...

POSSIBILITY
(its projections)

THROWNNESS
(that which ties-down its possibilities)

FALLENNESS
(its binding into the They-world)

All of this **matters** to *Dasein*, as the word "care" suggests (though it is not an ethical term). This "mattering" unifies *Dasein*. For Heidegger, care is the constellation in which *Dasein* has its being.

Something else matters: this constellation is **temporal**. *Dasein* is, **in time**.

So Heidegger set out to analyze TIME.

Philosophies of Time

Heidegger significantly re-formulated the usual Western concepts of time.

But what are these and how have they changed?

The COSMIC view as held by Aristotle

Time is the time of the natural world, readable from planetary motions and natural changes.

The THEOLOGICAL views of Christianity

*Time as given and ordered by God is finite or **eschatological**: it comes to an end.*

The SUBJECTIVE time of Descartes and the Enlightenment heirs

Time is something comprehended in the mind of a rational observer.

By the 1920s, modern "Cartesian" time had come under scrutiny. Heidegger had been reading the French "vitalist" philosopher **Henri Bergson** (1859-1941), and also Husserl, and both had attended to time.

Linear Time

Bergson's *Time and Free Will* (1889) distinguishes scientific knowledges of ourselves from our own experience of ourselves – a move with Heideggerean resonances.

Science, concerned with measurement, treats time *spatially*, as if it were a set of separable, quantifiable geometric units, like the spaces marked out on the dial of a clock (hours, minutes, seconds) or a calendar grid (days, months, years).

Science is also concerned with causes and effects. Time is therefore treated in terms of before and after, of earlier and later. Thus, time comes to rule as LINEAR TIME. **A** before **B** before **C** ...

The human experience of time is not scientific. Bergson describes it as a "flow" (*durée* or duration) involving past, present, future, and an experience of existing within that flow.

Bergson's Time

According to Bergson, "flow" resists measurement. It has no fixed norms or standards. We can experience a cinema film as "long" or "short", independently of and maybe **against** the measuring evidence of clocks. (Did we want it to go on longer? Regret the economic duty of sitting through it?)

In "flow", an experience in time becomes a past experience, and therefore something qualitatively different: it becomes a MEMORY...

...And future experiences, the not-yet, exist differently again: as imaginations or PROJECTIONS.

Experiences do not form a "line". A pressing future appointment, and a memory of other tedious films, can prolong a present film experience wonderfully.

"Flow" is resistant to calculation and objective measurement, mingling very particular sensations and memories. The experience of time as "flow" is unique to each individual. It might be partly communicable (e.g. in literature: Marcel Proust's novel of interior memory *A la recherche du temps perdu* was influenced by Bergson's ideas). But it is radically untransferable.

Husserl's Time-Consciousness

Husserl extended Bergson's work. He wanted to know how time "appeared" in consciousness: for example, in the ways that a musical melody might be known. A melody can be thought as a whole, complete from beginning to end, even on first hearing. But it is encountered in time, as successive separate notes.

*The melody is knowable only through the **simultaneous** operation of **three acts of consciousness** ...*

RETENTION: notes which are no longer sounding have to be retained, in memory.

ATTENTION: a "primal impression" of each note, as it sounds, must be gained.

PROTENTION: the auditor must "listen ahead", construct expectations of what might or might not follow.

Crucially, these have to occur together. Consciousness of time is a concatenation, a gathered-together-ness of future, past, present in protention, retention, attention. And that upsets the structures of LINEAR TIME: **A** before **B** before **C** ...

Time All At Once

Heidegger later quoted a letter of Mozart.

The composer describes how musical thoughts came to him "during a trip in a coach, or on a stroll after a good meal"...

"… soon one part after another comes to me, as though I were using crumbs in order to make a pastry according to the rules of counterpoint. Then it becomes ever larger, and the thing truly becomes almost finished in my head … so that afterwards I look over it with one glance in my mind, and hear it in the imagination not at all serially, as it must subsequently come about, but as though all at once …"

Mozart thinks a gathering of time – not linear, not clock-measurable. In this (and in the looking which is also a hearing) Heidegger finds "the essence of the thinking entrusted to us".

Time and Care

Much influenced by Bergson and Husserl, Heidegger in 1927 proposed that *Dasein* has its being in time. Its **horizon** is time.

First, time is structured into CARE.

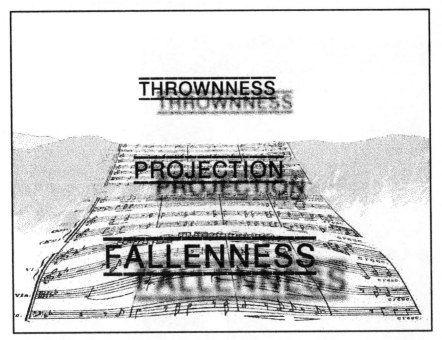

(1) **Thrownness** – *Dasein* is already in the world, dealing with what it receives from the *past*.

(2) **Projection** – living now its projections onto *future* possibilities, *Dasein* is always "ahead of itself". It is never entirely "all there at this moment" because its being encompasses its not-yets as projections.

(3) **Fallenness** – *Dasein* is pre-occupied with the world in the *present*, dealing with its concerns as they arise, in the particularized *nows* of the ready-to-hand and the Them-world.

Therefore *Dasein* fundamentally has its being in *all three* temporalities: its past, its possible futures, its present. Time is not lived fundamentally as quantifiable, geometric, linear time.

Mortality

Dasein is mortal. Death is the ultimate horizon, the condition in which *Dasein* is NO LONGER there. This presents difficulties.

If *Dasein* IS there, it is oriented to its future possibilities. But since they are **future** possibilities, then it is not all there, **yet**. It is incomplete.

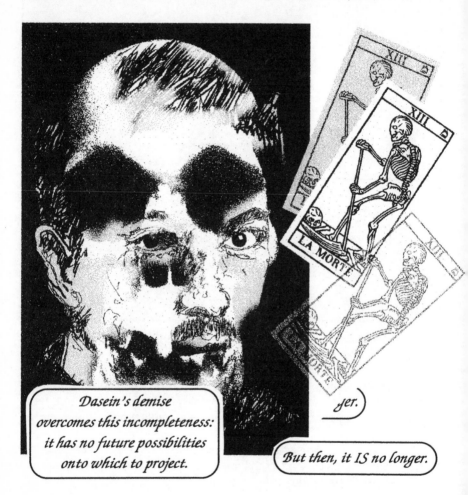

Dasein's demise overcomes this incompleteness: it has no future possibilities onto which to project.

But then, it IS no longer.

Heidegger escapes this logic by conceiving death as **one of the possible ways of being**. This seems strange. It threatens the logical prohibition of thinking "death within life".

Death Within Life

But if *Dasein* IS its not-yets, then its death is one of them (if a unique one). Its death is something it has to live, a future possibility (if a certain one) which is part of its present being. So, "death is a way to be". Usually, any such recognition collapses into fallenness.

In doing this, *Dasein* avoids the totality of its own life, its own being.

Time and History

Fundamentally structured in time, *Dasein* is uniquely and fully HISTORICAL.

Dasein is *Geschichtlich*, historical or history-ish, constituted by its pasts as well as present and futures. History-ish *Dasein* has its being in concern with the past. Note the distinction in German: *Geschichte* – the past as a historical reality; *Historie* – historical study, discourse on the past.

Heidegger is not interested in the "secondary historical", the past world registered as a list of things, more or less old. His interest lies with the "primary historical", which is *Dasein*.

Consider a museum...

"The 'antiquities' preserved in a museum (household equipment, for example) belong to a *'time which is past'* – yet they are still present-at-hand in the 'Present'. How far is such equipment historical, when it is *not yet* past?

Of course the tools have become fragile or worm-eaten. But that specific character of the past which makes it something historical, does not lie in this transience ..."

Heidegger's Museum of Household Utensils

What for Heidegger is the properly "historical"?

"What is 'past'? Nothing else than that WORLD within which the gear belonged to a network of equipment and was encountered as ready-to-hand by a concernful *Dasein* who was in-the-world. That **world** is no longer."

Heidegger reformulates *Historie*. Historical discourses usually treat the past as a set of objectified things or events. But *Dasein* exists as ***projective possibility***, not as a given, complete object. And *Historie* should be first and foremost the study of *Dasein's* dealings with its possibilities.

The past as Dasein's past projections is not lost.

The possibilities of the past can also be present and future possibilities, and the duty of a history is to reveal their power in the present. The task is to disclose *Dasein* in its repeatable historical possibilities. This is not history as the investigation of events, causes, effects, or collected facts.

Authenticity

In *Being and Time*, Heidegger proposes two basic ways that Dasein can be: **authentically** and **inauthentically**. The terms are from Søren Kierkegaard, the "first Existentialist". Kierkegaard equated WHOLENESS of human existence with authenticity.

AUTHENTIC being lies in the unifying of the scattered constituents of *Dasein's* being, including its being-towards-death. They have to be recognized for what they are, not lost in the practical world, not washed out by the Them.

So authenticity also means turning away from the everyday world and the Them.

In **INAUTHENTIC** being, *Dasein* takes up the tempting offer of a "home" in the world, with Them, and allows itself to find its security there. Thereby it closes off possibilities, sealing out *Dasein's* recognition of its unity.

But if everyday *being-in* and *being-with* is a fundamental mode of being for *Dasein*, how can *Dasein* escape it ?

Authenticity has to arrive out of the basic condition – inauthenticity. It will be a **modification** of inauthenticity. How? It arrives for instance in particular states of mind, and especially in ANXIETY.

Anxiety (*Angst* or dread from Kierkegaard) is unlike fear in that it has no specific object, nothing "out there" to be fearful *of*. For Heidegger it arises in *Dasein* itself, as an anxiety for its own being. *Dasein* experiences itself "called" into a disturbing awareness of that being.

Back to the homely reception of the familiar ready-to-hand things and the Them-culture. Back to the workshop and back to the dance halls.

In anxiety, *Dasein* is not at home, at all. In fact, Heidegger calls it the UNCANNY, the *unheimlich* or unhomely.

Such ideas were to have a powerful effect on currents in modern philosophy. The first prominent resonance: **Existentialism**.

Philosophers of Existence

Existentialists took up Kierkegaard's call for a philosophy centred on the "existing individual". Against rationalistic philosophical systems, they searched out the personal, subjective dimensions of human life: ethical or religious choice, emotional response, self-affirmation, committed action in the world.

In Germany, **Karl Jaspers** opposed the individual to mass society, and **Max Scheler** (1874-1928) interrogated human emotions and the will in interpersonal relations.

Both were read in France. But in the 1930s, it was Husserl and Heidegger who made the major impact on French philosophers.

Emmanuel Levinas (1905-95): studied at Freiburg 1928-9; first French exponent of Husserl and Heidegger; writer on time and death, but also ethics and the Other.

Paul Ricoeur (b. 1913): translator of Husserl's *Ideas*; phenomenologist and later theorist of literature and linguistics.

Gabriel Marcel (1889-1973): dramatist and writer of convoluted Existentialist diaries; critic of Cartesian rationalism and mind-body dualism.

By the 1950s, the word "Existentialist" had been popularized and applied to many things, from jazz to suicides. But the leading figures took emancipatory politics as a central concern.

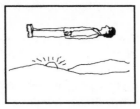

Maurice Merleau-Ponty (1908-61): Marxist phenomenologist 1930s-50s; Heidegger's being-in-the-world meant recovering lived material *experience* of the world, e.g. through perception and the body, even if such experience was fundamentally ambiguous and defied rationalist certainties.

Simone de Beauvoir (1908-86): influential critic of the "standard human being" as implicitly male; for de Beauvoir in the 1940s, existential freedom was gendered – being-as-a-female was not identical to being-as-a-male.

Jean-Paul Sartre (1905-80): novelist and philosopher, the most celebrated Existentialist; Sartre studied Husserl and Heidegger in Berlin, 1933-4.

Completing his reading of *Being and Time* in a wartime German internment camp, Sartre responded with *Being and Nothingness*, published in occupied Paris in 1943. A crucial Existentialist text, it has been described as "almost entirely an extended gloss on *Being and Time*".

Adventures in Humanism

But was *Being and Time* an Existentialist text, supporting Sartre's project? In 1946, Sartre argued that Existentialism was a **humanism**.

He did not mean a humanism which took "man" as something already given, complete in itself. Sartre redefined man as the "existential human subject", i.e. as a construction, constantly needing to be made: for instance, by "projecting" onto possibilities, struggling for "freedom" against the entrapping "situations" into which it is thrown, and by "engagement" – moral, ethical and political.

For Sartre, this existential human subject was philosophically central.

Man, projecting himself beyond himself, makes man exist. He himself is the heart and centre of this. There is no other universe except the human universe, the universe of human subjectivity.

Critique of Subjectivity

And Heidegger? He had no interest in placing "man" or even "existential human subjectivity" at the centre of anything. He was first an **ontologist**, not an Existentialist.

Being and Time had analyzed human being and adopted Existentialist terms (authenticity, angst, etc.), but only on the way towards being as such. Heidegger insisted that his work was not anthropological or anthropocentric – its central concern was not man or human subjectivity, but **being**.

In December 1946 he replied to a letter from Jean Beaufret, French Marxist and Existentialist – did he agree with Sartre's claims?

So being comes first.

Heidegger offers humanism a new-yet-more-fundamental meaning: no longer man as such, but **man in relation to being**.

For Heidegger, man is the "shepherd of being", attentive to being, guarding it – and in that lies the proper dignity of man.

Man in that sense comes before all concepts of humanism. It's a more __essential__ thought of man.

This is a radical disturbance of Western thinking about human subjectivity.

Heidegger refused to take man or subjectivity as an origin, a centre or a foundation on which to build a philosophy.

The bid was ambitious, perhaps unprecedented.
But wasn't the destruction of humanism a call towards *in*-humanity ?

Ethics and Values

Heidegger argued that he did not defend the inhumane or glorify "barbaric brutality" or promote a condition without values. "We should hold on to the rules that say how man should live in a fitting manner, however tenuously they hold human beings together."

However, the question of being has to come first — being is prior to all beings...

... If that displaces human beings or humane values from centrality, then so be it.

Critical opinions have been sharply divided. On offer is a radical re-opening of all questions of subjectivity – but also, Heidegger makes man as the "neighbour of being" more worthy of thought than man as the neighbour of man.

Questions of religion were not far away: Heidegger resisted Sartre's atheism. Did *Being and Time* carry theological implications?

Heidegger's Theology

The young Heidegger had immersed himself in conservative Catholicism: anti-modernist, authoritarian, deeply traditional and pre-occupied with decadence, sin, and fallen worldliness.

But he had failed to become a priest, a graduate theologian, or Professor of Catholic Philosophy at Freiburg, which had been his ambition in 1916, aged 27. In 1919, he had abandoned Catholicism.

A __questioning__ faith might more plausibly be Protestant...

Working with Husserl, a secular philosopher for whom God was "bracketed", Heidegger shifted again.

Philosophy is not faith...

...The philosopher does not __believe__ or behave religiously in philosophizing.

His comments on institutional religion became caustic.
It was the "shallow religiosity of our times", the "dreamstate of an occupation with sanctimony that one calls religion".

The Mistress and the Handmaid

Being and Time can therefore be read as a secular text. *Dasein* is announced as the universal structure of human being, grounded in no particular historical moment and no particular creed. *Dasein* is not Jewish, Christian, Buddhist, etc. It comes before these.

So, a final farewell to God? Not quite. Heidegger might have abandoned **theism** – some particular creator-god – but he never simply embraced **atheism**.

Through the 1920s he hoped to provide foundations for a renewal of Christian thought.

I supported the "Existential theology" of Rudolf Bultmann, the eminent Protestant theologian. For him, statements about God must become statements about the existence of man in relation to God.

When I go to the Bible the question to which I seek an answer... ...is the question of human existence.

Theology Demythologized

Aided by Heidegger's *Historie*, Bultmann "demythologized" Christianity. Biblical stories offered significant myths for people living in the world of the 1st century AD. But *that world* has vanished. So strip away those myths to reveal the fundamental, repeatable theological possibilities for believers now.

Out goes theology as a museum of religious utensils: "heaven" and "hell", "angels", "virgin births", etc...

"The cross" now reads "forgiveness" — "the resurrection" becomes "the new life"...

Theological debates helped to circulate Heidegger's work. But effectively, theistic readings put back what Heidegger had taken out. Although figures of "a god" and "the gods" were to return in strange ways to Heidegger's later texts, at the end of the 1920s he had quite different concerns.

Decision and Action

Heidegger returned to Freiburg in 1928, and took over Husserl's Chair of Philosophy. It was a turbulent period for the Weimar Republic: rapid inflation, stock market collapse, intensified political conflict. In July 1932, the National Socialist German Workers' Party became the largest elected party, and in January 1933 formed a government. The democratic Republic was dissolved.

Being and Time had a "decisionist" element: decisive action, seizing of possibilities.

A moment of decision seemed to arise.

In late 1932, Heidegger stood for election as Rector of Freiburg University, its chief regulative position. He was elected in April 1933, and on May Day 1933 he publicly joined the Nazi Party. Newspapers announced it without surprise.

"Heidegger with his care for the fate and future of the German people has stood in the heart of our magnificent movement. For years he has effectively supported the party of Adolf Hitler – no National Socialist has ever knocked in vain on his door."

Politics and Philosophy

Heidegger dismantled the University's democratic structures and called for radical curriculum reform, favouring philosophy. His many public speeches advocated loyalty to the Party, strong leadership and regenerated national identity.

1: *The German people must choose its future, and this future is bound to the Führer...*

...There is only one will to the full existence [Dasein] of the State. The Führer has awakened this will in the entire people...

2: *... we are only following the towering will of our Führer...*

...To be his loyal followers means: to will that the German people shall find again its ORGANIC UNITY, its SIMPLE DIGNITY, and its TRUE STRENGTH; and that it shall secure for itself PERMANENCE and GREATNESS...

...To the man of this unprecedented will, to our Führer Adolf Hitler — a three-fold "Sieg Heil!"

1: "German Men and Women!", *Freiburger Studentenzeitung*, 10 November 1933.

2: "National Socialist Education", in *Der Alemann: Kampfblatt der Nationalsozialisten Oberbadens*, 1 February 1934.

Heidegger adopted the Nazi rhetoric of *das Volk*, the "folk" or "people", declared as a national-racial "community". And he supported the Party's energetic appeals to "German youth".

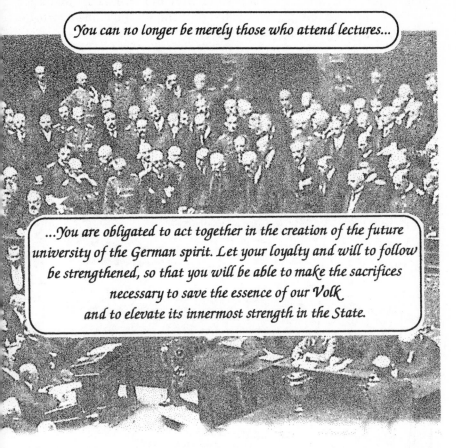

You can no longer be merely those who attend lectures...

...You are obligated to act together in the creation of the future university of the German spirit. Let your loyalty and will to follow be strengthened, so that you will be able to make the sacrifices necessary to save the essence of our Volk and to elevate its innermost strength in the State.

These were discourses of strident nationalist, militarist authoritarianism.

Dasein, conceived individualistically, had become the **German** *Dasein*. "Projection onto possibilities" became "choosing the path of greatness for the German people". "Seizure of authentic being" collapsed into "sacrificial loyalty to the Leader". Philosophy as commonly recognized was clearly not enough.

> "Let not propositions and 'ideas' be the rules of your being. The Führer alone is the present and future German reality and its law."

The Nazi Agenda

Launching into plans to transform the German university system, Heidegger held talks in April 1933 with the Prussian education ministry, sent two telegrams to Hitler personally, and made overtures to other Party educational reformers.

The Party's ambitions were perfectly clear.

JANUARY 1933:	Basic constitutional rights suspended.
FEBRUARY 1933:	Invocation of "emergency powers".
MARCH 1933:	Transfer of democratic parliamentary powers to the Nazi executive.
1 APRIL 1933:	Day of the Boycott: actions against Jewish businesses, academics, students, lawyers, doctors.
APRIL 1933:	Law to Restore the Professional Bureaucracy: removal of political opponents and "non-Aryans" from the civil service.
MAY 1933:	Political parties and trades unions liquidated or proscribed: union assets seized and socialist and Marxist parties outlawed.
DECEMBER 1933:	Law to Secure Unity of Party and Reich: the Nazi Party became the state party.
FEBRUARY 1934:	Law to enable all organizations and individuals to be placed under public control.
JULY 1934:	Centralization of the state security police, the SS; special courts to rule by "tenets of popular feeling".

By the mid-1930s, political opponents had been sacked, imprisoned or exiled, police powers had been centralized, mandatory "national workers' service" and military conscription were in operation.

It was a Party of *Gleichschaltung*, "harmonization". And from its inception in 1918, it had pursued racist policies which led by 1941 to the extermination camps and the murder of some 4,800,000 European Jews and many others.

The Politics of Renewal

Heidegger might not have held to the Party's programmatic anti-Semitism, but he supported its other trajectories. Labour, War and Education became a binding threefold imperative, a "primordial spiritual mandate of the German nation".

"University study must again become a risk, not a refuge for the cowardly. Whoever does not survive the battle, lies where he falls. A hardened race with no thought of self must fight this battle, a race that lives from constant testing …" ("The University in the New Reich", 30 June 1933.)

Marxist analyses of labour and social class had to be overcome.

* There is only one single German "estate". That is the estate of labour which is rooted in and born by the Volk and has freely submitted to the historical will of the State.

From 1929 to the mid-1940s, Heidegger conflated the favoured motifs of Nazism with his own philosophy.

* "Call to the Labour Service", for *Freiburger Studentenzeitung*, 23 January 1934.

Crisis and Nation

He adopted a prevailing conservative diagnosis of history. Modern society had reached a point of crisis, a traumatic turning point requiring resolute action. And what was at stake was the nation. Germany, unified in 1871 but condemned to pass through the "icy night" of 1918, had to seize its moment of spiritual renewal.

Heidegger knew for instance, Oswald Spengler's *Decline of the West*, a best-seller in 1919.

Out of an amorphous state of Culture will arise the true Civilization form, stabilizing and hardening in its final age...

...And it is Germany, as the central and last nation of the West, that will bring the final stage of Civilization to Europe, crowning the mighty edifice.

Germany has a unique place and a unique destiny. It is the centre of Europe itself ... where the destiny of the earth is being decided.

Germanness and Ruralism

"Germany" and "Germanness" are not very clear ideas, so philosophers laboured obsessionally to define them.

Heidegger had little interest in the usual strategies – embracing racist biologies, searching out essential German customs, and advancing empirical historical claims. He did, however, share in the appeals to *ruralism* ...

Nazism had annexed the ruralist repertoires of Neo-Romanticism: figures of the land, of Germany's fields and rivers, and of its *forests*, especially, with their deep-hidden but spiritually-regenerating sources, roots and mysteries.

Against the metropolitan city with its "inauthentic" masses was set the *Volk*, expressed in figures of organic life: the farmer, rooted in the soil, and the peasant *family*, as the sacrosanct centre of the people's life, hallowed by Christianity and by *völkisch* literature.

Rural Myths

Provincial peasant asceticism was part of Heidegger's self-image. To evade *das Man* in the 1920s, he wore a suit modelled on folk costume – tight trousers and a frock-coat. Aping more common professional practice, he built in 1922 a holiday home: a substantial stone-and-tile chalet clustered among others at Todtnauberg in the Black Forest. It has entered Heideggerean mythology as *die Hütte*, an isolated "peasant hut". Todtnauberg, on the hiking route but with death in its first syllable *Tod*, has been likened to the lair of Wagner's Alberich, "the dark of the dark of the dark, the most chilling remote place".

In a radio broadcast of 1934, Heidegger laid out his *völkisch* credentials.

"When, in the darkness of a winter night, a snow storm surrounds the shelter and covers everything, then the great moment of philosophy has arrived. Its questions must become simple and essential ..."

Philosophy in the Inglenook

Essential questions belong to essential thinkers.

"Philosophy is absolutely central to the work of THE PEASANT. The town-dweller thinks he is 'mingling with the people' when he deigns to have a long conversation with a peasant. When in the evening I interrupt my work and sit down on a bench by the fire or in the inglenook, then we often don't speak at all. We fall silent and smoke our pipes. ... The intimate rapport of my work with the Black Forest and its inhabitants is based on a priceless, age-old rootedness in the Alemanian-Swabian territory."

("Why do we prefer to stay in the provinces?", in *Der Alemanne*, March 1934.)

Underpinning Heidegger's "age-old" ruralism came another claim applauded by National Socialism: the German *language* was unique and coupled to German destiny.

Primordial Language

A cue had been provided by **Johann Gottlieb Fichte** (1762-1814), idealist philosopher, proto-nationalist and honorary forerunner of National Socialism.

A direct link exists between ancient Greek and German.

Other European languages are derivative of German or take their inheritance from a "dead" language, Latin.

Dead language, dead thinking: thought itself is corrupted, turned from its root, denied connection to the most ancient life-spring of European civilization...

...Properly philosophical thinking has to be German thinking.

For many philosophers, this established the Germans as the only remaining authentic and ancient people. And their destiny, their "world-role", was uniquely philosophical.

For Heidegger also, Greek was a "primordial" language – the most "original", that which comes first – and German had the direct line of descent. No deforming conduit troubled its route. Hence "only from the Germans can world-historical meditation come – provided that they find and defend what is German".

Were these nationalist motifs just superficial borrowings from a prevailing narcotic repertoire? Heidegger gave them a crucial twist. As he saw it, **the** destiny of the German nation had the **same** trajectory as his own highly distinctive philosophy.

The destiny of Germany towards "greatness" depends on gaining an "authentic knowledge of things" – i.e. it needs philosophy.

But which philosophy? Heidegger adopted a missionary and perhaps messianic role.

Nation, Crisis and Being

In Heidegger's view, German destiny *was* the recovery of the original, most primordial question: the question of being.

That meant contact with the Greeks, the "most primordial" of civilizations, and the German nation alone now possessed the sacred direct routes. Therefore a re-awakening towards being would ground the re-awakened German state.

"Nation" and **"crisis"** were bound together with *being* ...

The question of the meaning of BEING is primordial, and necessary if the PERIL OF WORLD DARKENING is to be forestalled...

...and if our NATION, in the centre of the Western world is to take on its historic mission.

So Heidegger projected himself as the philosophical leader of a National Socialist Germany.

It was an offer the political leadership could – and did – refuse.

In April 1934, his telegrams unanswered and his University reforms stalled by a professionally-affronted staff, Heidegger resigned the Rectorship and withdrew from explicitly political arenas.

However, he never openly disavowed the Party – apart from voicing some later doubts about its "technological" thinking.

Called in 1945 before De-Nazification tribunals at Freiburg, he concealed much of the history of his Rectorship, presenting it as a "failure" and its Nazism as a temporary career necessity.

Judged a fellow-traveller, he was suspended from teaching until 1951.

To many critics, there was one overriding scandalous fact. Heidegger after 1945 refused to pass judgement on National Socialism, even long after the horror and barbarism of the extermination programmes were known. He maintained a silence, in proper philosophical accord with the historical amnesia of the Adenauer era. (Konrad Adenauer, 1876-1967, first Chancellor of the new Federal Republic of Germany in 1949).

Political Controversies

Heidegger's texts have long circulated in this dusky political silence, in spite of critiques by German Marxists in the 1950s and 60s. But in 1987, research by Hugo Ott, Victor Farias and others internationally re-publicized the facts and added new ones. The debates since then have been extensive and vitriolic. The crucial question: was Heidegger's philosophy *inescapably* bound up with Nazist trajectories ?

From positions like that of Existentialist Karl Jaspers, "life" and "work" are inevitably intertwined.

Therefore the work is inevitably tainted – if one knows the facts of the political life, and considers them tainting...

But for other readers, life and work have to be distinguished. Therefore Heidegger has been defended: his political activism is purely a matter for biographers, political historians, etc. It is not a properly *philosophical* concern. And a text even by a declaredly Nazi philosopher can always be offered non-Nazi readings.

Some of Heidegger's critics have agreed. But they have suggested other links between his philosophy and politics.

Pierre Bourdieu (b. 1930), French sociologist, has seen Heidegger's philosophical *language* as political. He turned common words into special philosophical words and revived the ordinary meanings of learned words. Hence he can speak politically without appearing to do so.

Take the example of "care", **Fürsorge**. Once it becomes a philosophical word, any common notions of care, such as social care or welfare – **Sozialfürsorge** – are evaporated. Such moves carry a political charge.

For the Frankfurt School Marxist, **Jürgen Habermas** (b. 1929), *Being and Time* was an irreversible and profound turning point in German philosophy. But rejecting systematic study of politics and social life, Heidegger was prey to whatever political interpretations happened by.

Ill-considered and uninterrogated, his borrowings offered no resources for a *critical* view of Nazism – and that might remain true today.

Conservative Revolution

Other critics have read Heidegger's philosophy as "conservative revolution": a movement for radical change in the present through the rediscovery of lost truths of the past. Perhaps as in Heidegger's destructions: displace present meanings by reclaiming more original ones.

Something similar structured the discourses of Nazism. Crisis-ridden, it had to destroy the decadent traditions of the present, search out and restore the lost but true past, and thereby usher in the new dawn. In its rhetoric of the "return to order", Nazism appealed to principles outside of historical time: origins, sources, spiritual mandates, etc.

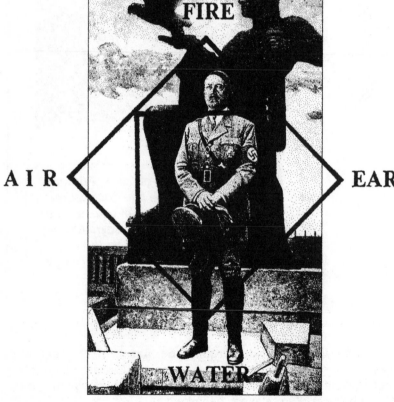

The similarity in their strategies ties Heidegger's philosophy to National Socialism, irrespective of any other known stances, statements, or biographical facts.

Questioning the Silence

Despite the force of these criticisms, Heidegger's work remained deeply influential on many who certainly have not shared his politics. Jean-Paul Sartre, a Marxist, is perhaps the most famous example; another is **Jacques Derrida** (b. 1930), whose ancestry is Jewish. But the most poignant case is that of the poet **Paul Celan** (1920-70), a Romanian Jew.

Both his parents died in the Nazi exterminations and he himself survived a labour camp. He wrote poetry in German which agonizingly tests the limits of that language – indeed, he too interrogates being, but from the perspective of the Holocaust.

So, how could he prize Heidegger's thought? How could he accept an invitation in 1967 to spend three days at Todtnauberg with the prince of the dark himself – a visit he later described as "most happy and productive"?

TODTNAUBERG

Arnica, eyebright, the
draft from the well with the
starred die above it,

in the
hut,

the line
– whose name did the book |
register before mine? –,
the line inscribed
in that book about
a hope, today,
of a thinking man's
coming
word
in the heart ...

These opening lines from Celan's poem reflect on Heidegger's constant, silent refusal to express any regret for his support of Hitler's regime. The poet still hopes for a "word" of some sort, as he signs Heidegger's guest-book.

Did Heidegger think that any word was needed? Perhaps he saw no error. And Celan, curiously, might have shared with Heidegger the sense of a question beyond talk of errors, atonement or regret; beyond the common currency of moral and political judgements – the question of being.

Arnica, a plant used as a remedy for bruises.   *Eyebright*, a plant used as a remedy for weak eyes.   The *starred die* is above Heidegger's well (see page 125).

The Truth of Being

How did Heidegger pursue this "question of being" after the political episode of 1934 and in the subsequent years? His exhaustive account of *human* being in the unfinished project of *Being and Time* had hardly addressed being *as such*.

Can I answer the question, "What is being?"

He had long known that *direct* answers would fail.

To say, *being is X or Y* ..., would turn being into *a* being, an X or a Y, just one more entity among others – and being as such would slip away again. Condemned to an oblique, circling approach, he asked: what is the TRUTH of being?

It scarcely sounds more helpful. But Heidegger thought there were TWO essential ways of arriving at truth. And one of them opened up a most unusual way of thinking about being.

Two Roads to Truth

Heidegger laid out the two roads to truth.

1. **ADEQUATION** or **CORRESPONDENCE**: statements and judgements must *conform* to an object, i.e. be like it or correspond to it in some way. Truth is the correspondence of knowledge to matter, of intellect to thing. If a statement does somehow "match" its object, it can be considered CORRECT or RIGHT – usually, "true".

What can be amiss with this rightness? It seems obvious, it's useful, and it doesn't even need God...

... But I have something else in mind ... aletheia.

2. **ALETHEIA** was the ancient Greek word for "truth". And according to Heidegger, it also meant UNCONCEALMENT. So when the Greeks thought of truth, they thought of unveiling, revealing, uncovering, or disclosing. Truth here is "bringing things out of concealment" – not matching up statements with objects.

The Truth of Truths

Heidegger argued that beings cannot be encountered, experienced and known as beings unless they are UNCONCEALED, i.e. disclosed, unveiled, etc. Statements and their objects are beings, and they cannot be "matched up" unless they are first disclosed as beings – along with the statement-makers. *Aletheia*, then, must come before adequation.

> *Aletheia is "first truth".*
> *It is truth as the most fundamental "coming into being" of beings.*

Across his entire later philosophy, Heidegger tried to describe this strange eventuation. *Aletheia*, unconcealment and disclosure were central terms.

However, they seem enigmatic. What did he mean by them?

Disclosures: from Husserl to Heidegger

Heidegger had already prepared his ground.

He took over archaeological metaphors from Husserl, who wrote of objects as "revealed" or "disclosed" in consciousness. And Husserl offered another powerful hint. Some objects were disclosed CLEARLY in consciousness, but some were in a "fringe" region, UNCLEAR or obscure – e.g. the "vagueness of a memory", the "unclear floating image of a fantasy".

Consciousness is a realm of both light and dark, yielding its flickering contents into clarity, or concealing them in shadow...

In *Being and Time*, entities are "disclosed" by *Dasein*. To disclose entities is to reveal them in particular ways, to encounter them, experience them or get to know them, as entities of this or that kind – e.g. as tools or natural things, as people or events, old or new, etc.

The Clearing

Disclosures need some *place* in which they can occur. In *Being and Time*, that place was *Dasein* itself. *Dasein* was a being that held itself "open" to beings. It was itself an "openness", a kind of "clear space" or "clearing", in which beings could be disclosed. Heidegger's terms were exotic, but effectively he modified a quite common notion: that it is **human beings** that encounter entities, turn them up, discover them, etc.

In the 1930s, Heidegger shifted *Dasein* from any possible centrality.

The "clearing" is now a field _beyond_ human being, and *Dasein* is _in_ it, along with all other entities.

It was an extraordinary move. What is this clearing? Heidegger calls it an "open region" or "field of relatedness" in which beings appear in many different ways, in mutual encounters with one another. Humans are important to it, but have no overarching mastery of what happens in it.

Opening, Lighting and Presencing

As such, this clearing is hard to grasp. It is not itself an entity, a thing, a substantial physical region, visible or audible. To describe it, Heidegger resorts to an abstruse, circling, hypnotically repetitive language.

"Clearing" in German is *Lichtung*, meaning an OPENING or open space. And it can mean a forest clearing, the place of a freeing, disencumbering spaciousness.

But *Lichtung* also means LIGHTING. So Heidegger uses metaphors of light – "clearing" in the sense of clarifying, bringing out of shadow or obscurity, lighting-up, illuminating.

And Heidegger writes of PRESENCING.

When beings are unconcealed, they become "present", i.e. they seem to be there with us, perhaps close by us, offering some kind of immanent contact with each other and with ourselves.

In the clearing, being conducts itself as a ***presencing***.

Why this strangely invented realm and this elaborate language for what we usually just call "reality" or "the material universe"?

Heidegger is out to disrupt common habits of thought. Ordinarily, we seem to live in a universe that is full up with all the things that exist – even if we overlook or misunderstand some of them.

But Heidegger's clearing is more like an infinitely complex space of **possibilities** for things and people to be. In it, some beings appear. But also, some **do not** appear. And if we neglect this **not** appearing, then in Heidegger's view we cannot understand the most fundamental events of being.

119

Concealment in Unconcealment

He puts the argument like this. *Aletheia* as unconcealment has an opposite: concealment. Beings that are "concealed" are not disclosed. And yet, very paradoxically, it is UNconcealment that produces this concealment.

How is this? To disclose a being in the clearing is to have it appear in a certain way, for example, as a "tool" or a "natural thing", as "decayed" or "dangerous", etc.

*But if the being appears **that** way...*

*... it's **not** appearing in some other way.*

Other ways **are possible**, but that particular disclosure, happening in its particular way, blocks them out. It conceals them.

Think of it like a radio. In tuning to one wavelength, we block out the others – they cannot be received at the same time, though they remain as unheard possibilities. Disclosing a being in one way, covers over its other possibilities. Every "unconcealment" conceals.

120

Limits of Disclosure

This has a historical dimension. Beings make their appearances differently in different epochs, and in some epochs they might not appear at all.

The ancient Greeks did not disclose DNA or human clones, nor a monotheistic God, Popes, witches and angels. And what the Greeks *did* disclose – in their slave-based economy, their Dionysian orgies, ritual ecstasies and appeals to myths and oracles – might now be lost, or scarcely accessible to us, with the loss of that epoch's *particular ways* of unconcealing.

And it is not possible to have *all* beings disclosed in the clearing, all at once. In fact, to think of *beings as a whole,* is to think of concealment and absence. Those that do not appear for us, and are not presences, are unimaginable *absences*.

The Hiding Light

Therefore the clearing is a most ambiguous realm, and not at all like a universe of stable presences. It is more like a field of flickering illumination and darkening. Beings appear in the light, but in that same light beings also retreat, slide into shadow, become absent. Every opening up closes, every lighting darkens – and in being's presencing, every presence arrives with absences.

For Heidegger, that is the truth of being: the play of the veiling-unveiling of beings. He finds it even in the word *aLETHEia* ...

... *lethe,* "concealment"...

... *hides inside unconcealment*...

And it has been noted most adroitly by the French psychoanalyst **Jacques Lacan** (1901-81).

In Heidegger's word *aletheia*, truth teaches her lovers her secret: that it is in hiding that she offers herself to them most truly.

Where does this leave philosophy? Heidegger's pursuit of being was also a sustained assault on Western philosophy. In his view, none of its great names – Plato, Kant, Hegel, even Nietzsche – had recognized the truth of being or found its language. In fact, their methods led to the **forgetting** of being.

*I set out to disrupt them,
along with all the habitual assumptions of science
and everyday thought.*

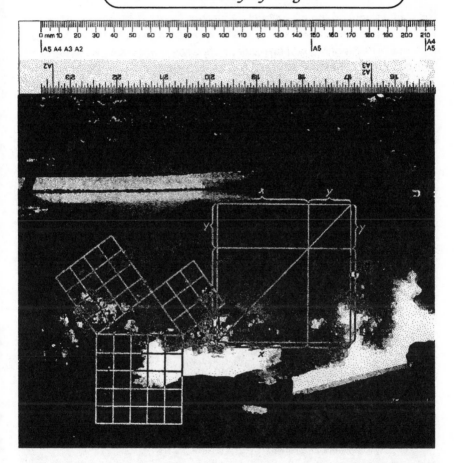

For instance, clearing, lighting and presencing defy any EMPIRICAL test. We cannot go and have a look at them, then compare what we find with Heidegger's statements. That would be seeking truth as adequation, and in Heidegger's terms, such verification is simply inapplicable – he cannot be said to be "right" or "wrong". *Aletheia* is not to be verified, it's to be *experienced*.

The Ruins of Logic

What about proofs by LOGICAL means?

Philosophers such as Heidegger's "Neo-Kantian" contemporaries had appealed to logic. Its statements were to be valid in all times and places, like those of mathematics: $17 + 1 = 18$, and neither time nor God can alter that in any way.

So, can we rely on the so-called Law of Non-Contradiction in logic, stating that something is either "A" or "not-A", and cannot be both at once? It offers a power of certainty, given any pair of opposed terms: something is *either* this *or* that, *either* light *or* dark, *either* present *or* absent, etc.

Heidegger wanted a different kind of power.

The concealing unconcealment, the obscuring clearness, obeys no law of logical opposition. Aware of the implications, Heidegger described concealment as *Geheimnis*, a mystery.

Towards "Thinking"

If truth is *aletheia*, then **truth is a mystery**: an echo of medieval and other mysticisms. Heidegger says this "disturbs philosophy", and in this he is at least correct.

He called for an overcoming of philosophy – the entire 2,500-year-old tradition that he summarized as "Western metaphysics". He renamed his own practice as a THINKING distinct from philosophizing. And this thinking was to be "intrinsically discordant", set against itself, because now it is responsible to both unconcealing **and concealing** ...

> *Philosophical thinking is gentle releasement that does not renounce the concealment of beings as a whole...*

> *... Philosophical thinking is especially the stern and resolute openness that does not disrupt the concealing but entreats its unbroken essence into the open region of understanding ...*

Thinking is a seduction of concealment.

Heidegger on Art

How was this thinking to proceed? Where is the **mystery** of being most evident, most fully experienced ?

Not where beings are very familiar...

Truth is never gathered from ordinary things that are at hand...

So Heidegger turned his attention to ART and POETRY. He explored the earliest Greek PRE-SOCRATIC philosophy, and also medieval MYSTICISM and NON-WESTERN philosophies.

His task was a strange one. He had to forge a mystic-poetic language that allowed and enticed the play of *aletheia*, a language with its own role in the eventuations of being as he saw them.

An important first move was to consider art. Heidegger's one major essay on art was delivered in public lectures at Freiburg, Zurich and Frankfurt, 1935-6.

It was a highly contentious and politically charged choice. A generation of Expressionists, Dadaists, Constructivists, New Objectivists and Brechtian realists had fractured the great traditions and challenged artistic values. But in 1933, the propaganda chief of the Nazi Party Joseph Goebbels and his Reich Chamber of Culture began "harmonizing" the artistic field.

Incorporating acceptable artists...

... and eliminating others.

It was not a simple task. Goebbels and others supported selected modernists, e.g. the "Nordic" Expressionists Nolde, Munch, Barlach and Kirchner – and some modernists were Party members.

The Nazi Attack on "Degenerate Art"

For four years, political authorities, curators and artists were locked in debate over German art.

By 1937, nine exhibitions had ridiculed "degenerate" art and modernist works had been banned from museums. Goebbels capitulated.
German art was now to be popular, easy to read, certain and clean – revived Neo-Classicism and Romantic *völkisch* naturalism: exalted landscapes, soil-rooted farmers, "Tyrolian youth" and "peasant Venuses".

Entering this contentious field, Heidegger claimed for art a specially compelling type of disclosure. In doing this, he made an important modification to his concept of "the clearing".

He identified in it two broadly distinct realms – WORLD and EARTH.

Realms of Being

The WORLD is the realm of human activity and relations, i.e. of human history: "the ever-changing realm of decision and work, of action and responsibility." This has usually been called "society" or "culture", but Heidegger was trying to find a more general and fundamental term that came before such names.

The EARTH is the realm of soil and rock, plants and animals etc., whose happenings are not those of human history or relations.

Earth extends beyond human historical time...

... and is not fully mastered by human decisions and choices.

Western science and philosophy have spoken of "the planet" or "physical matter" and especially "nature". But again Heidegger wanted to escape such thinking by conjuring a more fundamental term.

How are these two regions related? They take opposite sides in the play of *aletheia* ...

Essential Strife

- The world tends to be opening, to play to the light, to unconceal.
- The earth takes the side of closure, concealment, and also sheltering and preserving.

So the realms are in conflict, locked together in an essential STRIFE.

But the two sides of this strife are not absolutely distinct.

> *Earth mostly withdraws but will also rise up into the world...*

> *... for example, when humanly manipulated or named as "nature" ...*

And human decision and action is always based on, and drawn towards, something not fully mastered – the earth.

Such assertions might seem bizarre, even lunatic. To Heidegger they were necessary ways of escaping from traditional thought – and they seem less obscure if his sources are considered. He was drawing on the most archaic Greek philosophers, the **Pre-Socratics**.

Pre-Socratic Thinking

Active from 600 to 400 BC, the Pre-Socratics came before the "great" figures of Socrates, Plato and Aristotle. Their statements survive only in short isolated fragments, some less than five words long, and hard to interpret. Heidegger had been reading them since his student years.

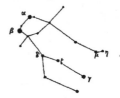

Mostly they offered __cosmological__ theories, explaining particular things – humans, plants, animals, planets and stars – but looking for an underlying unity in them...

Thales (c. 636-546 BC) thought that all things were forms of water...

For **Anaximenes** (c. 545 BC), they were air or mist...

And for **Anaximander** (c. 610-545 BC), they were "the Indefinite"...

Such thinking owed little to observation or experiment, but also, it did not rely on mythical gods or spirits.

Why was it attractive to Heidegger? Preceding philosophy as we know it, it seemed "more primordial". And it had not yet *forgotten* being.

Heraclitus

Heidegger wrote and lectured on **Parmenides** (c. 515-450 BC) and Anaximander. His notion of "strife" was taken from **Heraclitus**, active in Asia Minor c. 500 BC.

For Heraclitus, the three great cosmic components – fire, water and earth – are in constant flux. Each contains a cold moist portion and a warm dry one.

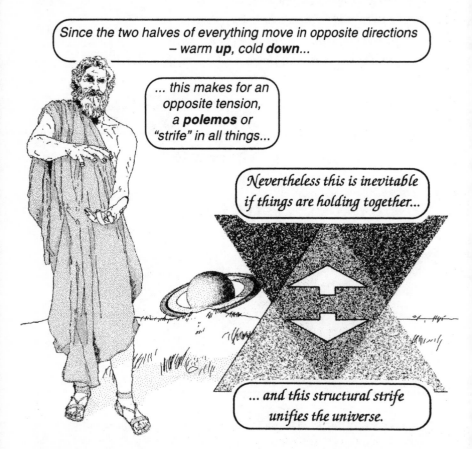

*Since the two halves of everything move in opposite directions – warm **up**, cold **down**...*

*... this makes for an opposite tension, a **polemos** or "strife" in all things...*

Nevertheless this is inevitable if things are holding together...

... and this structural strife unifies the universe.

A primitive mistake? Heidegger was attracted to the "hidden attunement" of all things paradoxically arriving as a conflict – like concealing unconcealment. And it offered a way of relating world and earth, his two realms of beings.

Apparently-stable reality occurs only in their strife...

The Work of Art

Where do works of art come in? Heidegger thought they had a special place in this world/earth strife.

In a peculiar way they belong to **both** realms at once. They are not like stones or rain – "natural" things that belong to the realm of EARTH. But also, they are not like practical "equipment-type" things – like shoes which belong to the human WORLD.

Art works are a kind of interface site, a meeting place of human purposes and decisions, and their un-masterable, non-human horizon.

When art works disclose entities, they bring the meeting of earth and world to our attention...

What Do Shoes Disclose?

He took shoes as an example. Shoes are disclosed as equipment-type things just by using them. So, surely, they could not also be disclosed in a *painting* of shoes – one, say, by **Vincent Van Gogh** (1853-90)?

And yet, perhaps they could be disclosed *differently*. In 1930 Heidegger had seen in Amsterdam one of Van Gogh's eight paintings of shoes: perhaps "Old Shoes" (1886). Inventing a female peasant owner, Heidegger finds the shoes belonging to the EARTH ...

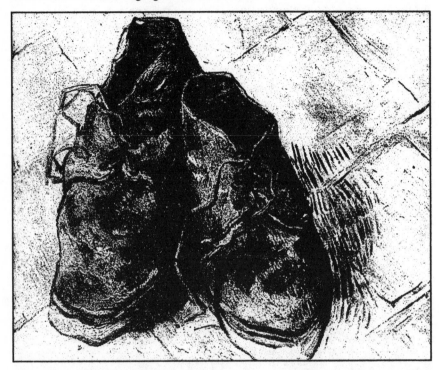

"From the dark opening of the worn insides of the shoes the toilsome tread of the worker stares forth. There is the accumulated tenacity of her slow trudge through the far-spreading furrows of the field swept by a raw wind. On the leather lie the dampness and richness of the soil. Under the soles stretches the loneliness of the field-path as evening falls. In the shoes vibrate the silent call of the earth, its quiet gift of the ripening grain, the fallow desolation of the wintry field."

And in the same resonant *völkisch* prose, the shoes find their place in the human WORLD.

> "This equipment is pervaded by uncomplaining worry as to the certainty of bread, the wordless joy of having once more withstood want, the trembling before the impending childbed and shivering at the surrounding menace of death ..."

Therefore its **depicted shoes** are disclosed as belonging to the earth **and** the world – unlike actual shoes, disclosed purely as equipment of the world. Hovering between the world and the earth, the art work enacts the essential strife, bringing it to attention.

The Temple

Another example is the Greek temple.

The temple establishes the WORLD – the users' history, their sense of time, religious practices, etc. But it also belongs to the EARTH. The temple "rests on the rocky ground" and stands against sky, storm, light, sea and surf, making these manifest, making them "appear as what they are"...

"The building holds its ground against the storm raging above it and so first makes the storm itself manifest in its violence. The lustre and gleam of the stone brings to radiance the light of the day, the breadth of the sky, the darkness of the night. The temple's firm towering makes visible the invisible space of air. Its own repose brings out the raging of the sea."

In the temple, world and earth enact their mutual interfacing.

Art at Work

Heidegger's treatment of art is surprising. Effectively, he **redefines** it. "Art" now means: the enactment of essential strife, the happening of truth at work.

His essay has been much debated and there are many problems. For instance, Heidegger says he deals only with "great art" – but how can we tell which art that is?

Are we bound to his politically resonant examples? A "conservative revolutionary" painter, who mapped ruralist myths to Expressionist modernism? ... A building embedded in the Nazi mythology of Aryan-Greek primordiality? Could the essential strife of being shine equally, say, in Andy Warhol's "Diamond Dust Shoes" of 1980? ...

Or any depicted shoes?

The debates continue. But for Heidegger, the crucial move was to lodge his vocabulary of "being" in a site more hospitable than philosophy, science or everyday thought. Art provided that site.

The Names of Poetry

Heidegger's argument seems to privilege visual art, but he emphatically maintained that *linguistic* works were paramount. They NAME.

In Heidegger's sense, beings cannot appear in the clearing without words. Language essentially names everything that is and its characteristics, and in a sense grants being to entities. Before a name ("feminism" or "the unconscious", "client-server architecture" or "Neo-Heideggereanism"), entities might appear – but not in the ways that *that* name specifically allows.

Names establish beings and "keep" them.

> Naming is a _Verhältnis_ – a holding together, a vouchsafing or granting...

> ... But names can be lost, too.

Heidegger described this as "poetry". It is not just any language use, and especially not practical communication, but rather a passage of "essential" words, attuned and responsive to being. "Poetry" took on a privileged position in Heidegger's thinking.

Heidegger was searching for an ***essential language***, a "poetry" that could speak of being. Poetry in the ordinary sense – literary verse – had an important role.

Heidegger acknowledged a conventional list of the classics, noting Homer, Sophocles, Dante, Virgil, Shakespeare and Goethe. Contemporary poets also figured – not just Paul Celan, but Neo-Romantic writers like **Rainer Maria Rilke** (1875-1926), and Expressionist modernists **Stefan George** (1868-1933) and **Georg Trakl** (1887-1914).

Among their concerns were immanent experience and the life of the spirit in the modern era...

HÖLDERLIN
1770-1843

But one figure came first: **Friedrich Hölderlin** (1770-1843), prototype German nationalist, Hellenizer of Romanticism and paganizer of Christian theology.

Legacies of Hölderlin

Rediscovered by Dilthey in the 1860s, re-published in the 1910s, Hölderlin's poetry arrived "new" but not modernist. In richly allusive verse, Greek forms and motifs met the themes of Romanticism – especially "the Poet" as solitary seer.

And Hölderlin invented a theology of "lost gods".

The deities known to the ancient Greeks have departed, but a New God might one day appear...

All of the poet's thinking was held under the spell of Heraclitus.

Heidegger wrote five essays on Hölderlin and often quoted him. He seemed to explore essential naming and realms of being: world, earth and also gods.

So Heidegger felt that Hölderlin was one who **knew being**. Bypassing standard philosophical argument, Heidegger needed this unique, poetic authority.

Remembrance of the Poet

Hölderlin's 1802 poem "Homecoming" tells of a poet's journey across the Alps to his German homeland, Swabia. In 1944, Heidegger's essay "Remembrance of the Poet" elaborated Hölderlin's themes.

In the Alps, the poet finds a joyous spirit of homecoming ...

... an immanent spirit comes, and a joyous courage swells again ...

For Heidegger, this becomes THE JOYOUS, spoken in words of light: "It is the calm mien which everything has in greeting the seeker. Everything that is openly friendly, light, gleaming, shining and bright ..."

But above even the light is a kind of essential Joyousness, THE SERENE – that which places, orders, and clarifies everything, according to the proper nature of its existence: "a pure lighting, a streaming lighting, conferring brightness on the light itself."

The Serene is also the HOLY. So in this highest realm is a god ...

... higher up still above the light there dwells the pure Blissful god rejoicing in the play of holy beams...

Here dwells the "high one", who is who he is; the Joyous ONE, the high father heaven (if he is a person)...

Sliding behind these titles, the god is elusive, withdrawing. Its essential name has not been granted, it cannot yet appear in the clearing.

But a new Trinity is possible. "The wafting *Air*, the clarifying *Light* and the *Earth* which blossoms with them are the *'three in one'*."

Hölderlin is offered an ethereal architecture: from the High ONE, a LIGHTING is sent through the Joyful SERENE, which dispatches its GREETINGS to illumine the SPIRIT OF MEN...

And messengers are needed, i.e. heralds or Angels ...

Come, ye preserving ones! Angels of the Year! And ye,
Angels of the House, come! ... So that no human good, no
Hour of the day may be fittingly hallowed
Without the Joyful Ones ...

Heidegger's **Angels of the House** are angels of the EARTH: the house is the "space which men need, to be at home" – a space given by earth.

The **Angels of the Year** are angels of the LIGHT, therefore of time, the **changing** of the Serene, "meting out the time of historical sojourn in the house".

And for Heidegger, as for Hölderlin, it is the POET, coming "first and therefore alone", who alone can respond to these greetings and tell others.

143

The One... the Holy Serene... the Angels and the Poet – what is Heidegger trying to name? It seems a strange text for a philosopher "central to European thought".

Heidegger was forging a secular theology and a philosophical poetics simultaneously. Hiding in the ruins of the pagan *and* the Christian, his divinity fits no orthodox religion. Like Hölderlin, he calls for the new god, while lacking any name: no obvious, used-up name – Christian or otherwise – can usher it towards us. But why is it needed?

The essential words – the ones that name, or establish being – must be constantly related to "the one and the same": a point of singularity.

This has to be understood as "perpetual and permanent" – it comes before anything changeable. His notion of "the divine" fulfils that role.

The Journey

Hölderlin also seems to know the mystery of being – the paradoxical veiling and reserving that accompany revealing, and which can leave logic in disarray. To reach Swabia, the poet has to leave the Alps, so surely he is *leaving* his gladdening proximity to the Most Joyous ?

Not for Heidegger …

"Proximity is *not* the smallest possible measurement of distance between two places. Proximity makes the Near near, and yet at the same time the sought-after, and therefore the not near. Proximity consists in bringing near the Near, *while keeping it at a distance*. Proximity is a mystery. "

The near is both close *and far*. As *far*, it is reserved, withdrawn, concealed...

... but it must *stay* partly concealed, or it will cease to be the near. In this lies its mystery.

The Homecoming

Heidegger finds in this "proximity" the essence of home and homeland. Germany is no mere geography, but the contemplation of a "source" which is both close and far.

"The innermost essence of homeland – all that is German – is **reserved**. Those who are far away yet sacrifice their life lavishly for the still-reserved discovery, might be the nearest kindred of the poets. Then there is homecoming. This homecoming is the future of the historical being of the German people."

Heidegger's Germany is readable at least twice: as a Germany of the nationalism of 1944, stitched to the war effort; and also as a scarcely possible Germany – a never-yet, a close-but-far, a mystery of proximity, a "source" to be sought after, but guarded as something reserved.

The Four-Fold

After 1945, Heidegger abandoned overtly nationalistic motifs. But he continued to explore language and poetic thinking, often modifying his ideas about the regions of being.

In 1951, he introduced the FOUR-FOLD, *das Geviert*. This is a unified interplay or "happening together" of earth, sky, mortals and gods.

> "Recall that human being consists in dwelling - in the sense of the stay of mortals on the earth. But 'on the earth' already means 'under the SKY'..."

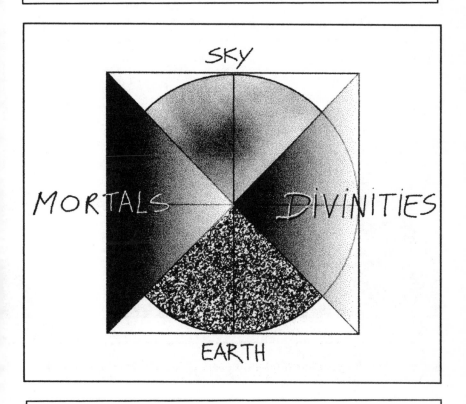

> "... Both of these also mean 'remaining before the divinities'. By a *primal* oneness, the four – earth and sky, divinities and mortals – belong together in one."

Clues to this interplay came from Hölderlin – for instance in his poem "Bread and Wine" (1800). The gods of a poetic ancient Greece are called upon by mortals, yet have withdrawn.

> "The thrones, where are they? Where the temples, and where the vessels, where, filled with nectar, fit to please gods, is song? Delphi slumbers, and where does the great destiny sound?"

The gods leave a "mourning earth" and a few gifts. "Bread is the fruit of earth, but is blessed by the light, and from the thundering god comes the gladness of wine."

And between the gods and mortals, there is LANGUAGE: the passing of the essential words.

> "The word's power increases, and far as it can travel, the ancient sign handed down from forebears, striking, creating, resounds. … Night grant us the onrushing word which will be sleepless like lovers."

148

Heidegger's Four-Fold is a simple unity, so to think of each realm is to think of the others. He describes them in Hölderlinian fashion.

"The EARTH is the serving bearer, blossoming and fruiting, spreading out in rock and water, rising up into plant and animal ..."

"The SKY is the vaulting path of the sun, the course of the changing moon, the wandering glitter of the stars, the year's seasons and their changes ..."

Frugiferas aruis fert Aestas torrida meßeis .

"The DIVINITIES are the beckoning messengers of the godhead, out of whose holy sway the god appears or withdraws into his concealment ..."

"The MORTALS are human beings: they can die. To die means to be capable of death *as* death. Only man dies."

Language, too, has a part to play ...

Attunement and Gathering

This is no longer language as practical communication, nor as the words and rules studied in scientific linguistics. Heidegger is resolutely displacing ordinary thought.

In his view, language is *impersonal* and not merely the property of human beings. It belongs to the Four-Fold. This is hard to grasp, but consider that when an orator speaks, it is *language* that does the work, makes the meanings, etc.

Language speaks, not the orator – and it comes before the orator, speaking the orator's name and identity...

LANGUAGE "SPEAKS US",
NOT VICE VERSA...
AND IT "SPEAKS" ALL
OTHER BEINGS...

LANGUAGE "SPEAKS US",
NOT VICE VERSA...
AND IT "SPEAKS" ALL
OTHER BEINGS...

LANGUAGE "SPEAKS US",
NOT VICE VERSA...
AND IT "SPEAKS" ALL
OTHER BEINGS...

In Heidegger's sense it holds the Four-Fold together, keeping the face-to-face encounters of the regions in *attunement* or harmony. And it performs an *original gathering* or collecting together of the regions.

Another kind of *gathering* is performed by buildings – e.g. a bridge. First, EARTH...

The bridge does not just connect banks that are already there. It is one particular way of "making the banks emerge" as banks.

The bridge brings the stream and the bank and the land, into each other's neighbourhood...

...The bridge *gathers* the earth as landscape around the stream.

The SKY too is gathered...

"The sky's floods from storm or thaw may shoot past the piers in torrential waves. The bridge holds the flow up to the sky, by taking it for a moment under its vaulted gateway and then setting it free once more."

Heidegger displaces the usual assumptions: *first* there is a landscape, *then* a bridge is superimposed on it – as if we have to mime in thought the sequence of geological formation and technical construction.

It's rather that a building – in this instance a bridge – offers its surroundings a being of a certain kind, which they *could not have* without it. It's a *simultaneous* disclosure.

Earth and sky achieve their presences *with* the bridge, in the particular way the bridge gives.

And the mortals and gods?

The bridge "grants the way for mortals to cross it", in daily business, while connecting mortals to divinities – perhaps in an aspirant "vaulting" over human "commonness and unsoundness" – perhaps in meditation on the divine.

Is it then merely a bridge... or a little after that, some cultural symbol? It remains only a thing, yet gathering the Four-Fold.

Departing From the West ?

This is not the standard fare of Western philosophy. Heidegger was exploiting many sources, including Eastern thought. He became familiar with Buddhist and Taoist texts in the 1920s and 30s, assisting in translations and borrowing themes or even whole passages for his own writings.

There are many points of contact. Buddhism and Tao have stressed **non-dualistic** thinking – no subject-object distinctions, no simple oppositions. Thinking is turned towards the **impermanence** or insolidity of entities, not towards stable substances...

*And unlike Western scientific reason, explanations are not sought in terms of **cause and effect**...*

So Heidegger's Four-Fold has Eastern parallels.

Michael Zimmerman, for instance, finds echoes of it in a story from the Buddhist Hua-Yen thinkers ...

The Jewel Net of the God Indra

The god Indra has a net of infinite expanse, representing the universe, and in it are set an infinite number of perfect gems, each of which reflects the light given off by all the others.

This light plays mutually and simultaneously between all of them – no one object has priority or superior position...

Heidegger's Four-Fold shares at least some of this.

Entities appear simultaneously together, in a mutual interplay within a poetically-spoken arena. Metaphors of lighting and luminosity describe their moment-by-moment manifestation. And their play is causeless, having neither ground nor reason.

The Principle of Reason

Heidegger also made use of Western mysticism. From 500 AD to the 1300s, Christian mystics had sought an ecstatic spiritual union or one-ness with God. God was beyond all conceptual categories and rationalizing proofs, but might be personally experienced through "humility" or "poverty" – the dissolution of the self and the everyday world – and through reflective contemplation of divine illumination.

Heidegger had long known the works of the medieval mystic **John (Meister) Eckhardt** (c. 1260-1328) and others which offered an alternative to philosophical reason.

In 1955, he identified the key modern sense of "reason" in a phrase by **Gottfried Wilhelm Leibniz** (1646-1716). And he set against it the mystical thinking of **Angelus Silesius** (1624-77) ...

Reason and Being

Leibniz [*] claims that every fact must have a "sufficient reason", explaining why it is so and not otherwise. He seeks a "why" and a "cause". The being of Angelus' rose will not open itself to that search.

Heidegger appeals also to Heraclitus: *reason* belongs intimately together with *being*.

However, later conceptions of reason, as "ratio" or logic, have pushed this aside.

[*] Gottfried Leibniz: Rationalist philosopher and mathematician

The Play of Being

For Heidegger, being occurs as a causeless, groundless *play* – a play more reasonable to Angelus and Heraclitus than Leibniz and the moderns: the "play in which humans are engaged throughout their life, that play in which their essence is at stake." Heraclitus makes this point …

Time is a child playing draughts... the kingly power is a child's...

The destiny of being ? A child that plays, shifting the pawns...

Why does it play, the child of the "world-play" Heraclitus brought into view ? It plays, because it plays. The "because" withers away in the play...

"The play is without 'why'. It plays since it plays. It simply remains a play: the most elevated and the most profound. But this 'simply' is everything, the one, the only..."

Words and Writing

Heidegger had other strategies for disrupting standard thought. He explored his own language, making German foreign to itself while returning it to its more original possibilities. He searched out hidden *etymologies*, historical meanings of words – most usually, lost senses of "being".

For instance, *bauen* means "building", i.e. technical construction. But in Old German it also meant cultivating, nurturing, caring and preserving...

Words related more closely to __being__ than to technically constructing something...

The modern sense of bauen forgets this.

BAUEN

In such words there is now an unheeded silence...

Words get used up, become commonplace, lose their power of granting being. Heidegger wanted to restore this capacity to them.

He mobilized strange writing styles, personal spellings, obsolete words, new coinages and words with multiple resonances. These were attempts to regenerate language.

Even the word of being, *Sein*, gets worn out. And Heidegger said he got tired of it. He sometimes resorted to an archaic spelling, *Seyn*.

In his essay "*Zur Seinsfrage*", he crosses it out. [S̶e̶i̶n̶]. It has to be used, but it cannot be allowed simply to represent being...

A representation of being, in word or otherwise, is not being...

... So its word-ness is removed...

To many linguists, Heidegger's etymologies have seemed fanciful, and his unorthodox writing has troubled many philosophers.

To Heidegger, they were ***necessities of thinking***.

Technology and Modernity

A major "necessity of thinking" was the critique of technology. Long influenced by anti-modernisms, Heidegger identified in the 1950s and 60s a "limitless domination" of modern technology.

He offered important criticisms. A measuring, reckoning, calculating logic is applied to everything. Human activity is to be governed by **efficiency** – maximum output for minimum input. Nature is to be commanded and manipulated.

Technological thought sets no limits to itself...

...It is infinitely expandable and erodes other modes of thought.

Hence an unrestrained, complete technicizing of the world and of humans. Even human discourse will be consigned to "electronic thinking and calculating machines", circulating "information" as an end in itself.

The Lost Meanings of Techne

Heidegger also searched out the lost meanings of "technology". In the 1830s, it came to mean scientific thought applied to manufacturing. But it derives from the Greek word *techne*.

Techne not only meant the activities and skills of a craft worker, but also the "arts of the mind" and fine arts...

Techne also contained something poetic, that is, something of *poiesis* ...

Poiesis in Greek meant bringing-forth, or bringing into presence – and this happens in all craft manufacture and all arts.

Techne and *poiesis* are words of *aletheia*, of fundamental disclosure. Modern "technology" has lost this meaning. Technology does "disclose", but in a way that *obliterates poiesis*.

Technological Disclosure

Technology operates as DISPOSING, not *poiesis*. Disposing reveals things as things which are completely **available**. Entities are disclosed as fully available for use, extraction, manipulation, etc.

Everything therefore becomes a STOCK, a fund or supply, ready and waiting. In the technological age, stock is taken simply as "what is real".

And disposing means a CHALLENGING-forth, a SETTING-UPON nature:

"Agriculture is now the mechanized food industry. Air is now set upon to yield nitrogen, the earth to yield ore, ore to yield uranium. Uranium is set upon to yield atomic energy. This setting-upon unlocks and exposes, driving on to the maximum yield at the minimum expense."

The Danger of Technology

Technology, then, *is* a mode of disclosure. But to reveal beings technologically is to coerce, compel, provoke or harness them – making them appear as stock.

The peril of this? *Poiesis* is shrivelled. The primordial Greek modes of disclosure are blocked. So Heidegger does not find the danger of technology in this or that set of machines or techniques, nor in particular uses of them, nor in reckoning up social or environmental damage...

The true danger is that technology leads mankind even further from being.

He offers a solution.

Poiesis might lie concealed *inside* technological disposing, because disposing remains a type of disclosure. *Poiesis* hides there as a "saving power".

The only hope, Heidegger suggests, is to entice its emergence.

Saving Power

How can this "saving" be done? Only through reflective thinking and perhaps art. The fine arts, "called to poetic revealing", akin to technology but fundamentally different from it, might foster a newly poetic *techne*.

This might seem impractical and quietistic, even passive. Heidegger called for a "letting-be", a reflective attunement to being.

*No **action** of the usual kind can help. Action is already bound into technology.*

Surprisingly, this thinking has influenced ecology – or at least some "deep ecology".

Founded by **Arne Naess** (b. 1912) in the 1970s, deep ecology proposed an intrinsic value in non-human entities, and therefore restraint in human practices. And its many mutations have embraced consciousness-raising, nature mysticisms, pantheistic religiosity, naïve animism and cosmic identification ("you are the planet").

Ecology and Essential Thinking

Put carefully, Heidegger's thinking offers ecology a philosophical alternative to calculating rationalism.

Some have used it to undermine Man-Nature dualisms and the ecological centrality of Man. It has lent itself to holistic and contemplative approaches, and to the critique of technical solutions, such as "environmental management".

And yet, almost none of this was Heidegger's concern. He wasn't saving the planet *or* trying to improve the conditions of life or non-life on it. His problem was the "forgetting of being".

As he saw it, technology was related to a HISTORY OF BEING...

A history of how "being" received its names in the Greek, medieval and modern epochs...

...What needs safeguarding in this is the *essence of humanity* – its proper bearing towards being...

The History of Being

In Heidegger's history, being has been named as *Idea* (Plato) or *Substance* (Aristotle), as *God* and as *Subject* (Descartes), and *Consciousness* (Husserl) – and others have contributed, such as Nietzsche with his "Will to Power".

This is a history of "metaphysical" Western thought. In it, **being** is progressively forgotten, or rather, withdraws itself. Once Plato, or maybe earlier Anaximander, had set out towards reason, calculation, and proofs by logic or observation, being was sent off towards the possibility of oblivion.

It is the final stage of the **oblivion of being** – unless a non-metaphysical **and** non-technological thinker can speak the danger and be heard.

The Essential Question

Heidegger's critique of technology is neither a simple anti-modernism, nor a programme for ecological politics. It is couched more "essentially".

This has raised some typical problems. Thinking "essentially", Heidegger deploys unthought images of reactionary pastoralism and rural nostalgia. And he offers no economic, social, political or ethical arguments. These belong to completed metaphysics or technology, so he turns away from them. There is only *one* crucial question ...

"Humans are the *reckoning* creature. Does this exhaust the essence of humanity? Or isn't human nature, its affiliation to being, and the essence of being, what still remains worthy of thought? That is the question. It is the world-question of thinking. Answering this question decides what will become of the earth and of human existence on this earth."

Heidegger's Influence

Heidegger's own claim to significance lies grounded in that one question – the question of being.

However, what Heidegger did *on the way* towards being is also significant. He proposed an extraordinary meeting of Greek, medieval and modern philosophy, the far-reaching concepts of *Dasein*, world and time, and the disturbance of most ordinary thought about art, poetry and language. Heidegger's thinking skirts the edges of the thinkable – and his strategies for overcoming three millennia of Western philosophy have proved widely attractive.

So, Heidegger's influence has been widely *dispersed*, and it often turns up in projects unconcerned with his question of being. To take one notable field, it is found in "post-structuralist" thinking, especially in France.

Some Post-Structuralists

Michel Foucault (1926-84) studied Heidegger intensively in the 1940s and 50s.

I put to use Heidegger's critiques of subjectivity and Cartesian rationalism – but in theories of power, knowledge and discourse.

Jacques Lacan (1901-81) translated Heidegger and made a pilgrimage to Freiburg in 1950.

I exploited Heidegger's concepts of temporality, thrownness, language and "the real" – but in psychoanalysis.

*Like philosopher **Gilles Deleuze** (1925-95), they took on Heidegger's <u>conceptual strategies</u>, rather than his particular concern for <u>being</u>.*

Likewise **Jacques Derrida** (b. 1930) and "deconstruction". Derrida has acknowledged a profound debt to Heidegger. But his readings are not Heideggerean, if that means pursuing being. Derrida's interest is the radical disturbance of Western metaphysics.

Heidegger's Deconstruction

In fact, Heidegger's notion of being remains locked in the metaphysical tradition. Heidegger, not Nietzsche, is the last metaphysician – he still clings to the search for metaphysical *foundations*, for essences, origins and truth.

Derrida interrupts this search with devices borrowed from Heidegger. For instance, he disrupts "oppositional" thinking, and that includes Heidegger's founding opposition – *beings / being*.

How might we think, once even the deepest sedimented foundations of thought are disturbed? ...

...In this, Heidegger is crucial – but he is deprived of the assured centrality of "being".

From other perspectives – e.g. that of pragmatist philosopher **Richard Rorty** (b. 1931) – Heidegger constructs a *myth* of being. And there are other myths we might do without...

Demythologizing Heidegger

John Caputo, for instance, has proposed "demythologizing" Heidegger – for example, by scrutinizing his myths of German-Greek inheritances, single primordial origins, and *aletheia* as a privileged possession of the Greeks.

Caputo suggests disturbing the "power, glory, and prestige of *being*" – with the "poverty, invisibility, and humility of *justice*". This is one of many bids to re-introduce social, political, and ethical questions.

Jewish philosopher **Hannah Arendt** (1906-75), student and close associate of Heidegger, is just one who has found his "essential" thinking insensitive to particular human *differences* – for instance, those of racial identities, and also perhaps of gender.

However, all these readings *engage* with Heidegger's thinking rather than dismiss it. Yet Heidegger has also attracted many scholars who have safeguarded his thinking almost as "faith".

Heidegger's Question

From Heidegger's perspective, radical movements in thinking had only one essential task – to pursue the question of being. It arrived as the only question worthy of thought.

But as we have seen, the question had no "answer" in the usual sense, only continual reformulations: the *meaning* of being, the *truth* of being, the *regions* and *events* of being.

Writing of *aletheia*, the clearing, the Four-Fold and language, he never treated any of them as settled concepts.

Rather, I hoped that others would take them up and pursue them, along with my most insistent call...

– the call for a new disposition towards being, and a new, scarcely-imagined, human responsibility...

"We are the ones bestowed by and with the clearing and lighting of being, and accordingly the same ones that being touches in, and by, its withdrawal.

We stand in a clearing and lighting of being. We stand in it as those who are claimed by the being of beings. We are the ones bestowed, the ones ushered into the time play-space.

That means we are the ones engaged in and for this play-space; engaged in building on and giving shape to the clearing and lighting of being – in the broadest and multiple sense; in preserving it.".....

Will Heidegger's thinking prove most influential as a re-examination of Western thought, or as a fundamental re-awakening towards being?

So far, the former looks more likely.

Heidegger, I believe, most fervently hoped for the latter.

Bibliography

Heidegger's collected works, fully published, will amount to some 100 volumes, and writings about Heidegger run into many thousands. The most complete list to 1972 is Hans-Martin Sass's **Martin Heidegger: Bibliography and Glossary** (Bowling Green State University, Ohio, Philosophy Documentation Centre, 1982). Useful introductory lists are in Guignon and Krell below, and Thomas Sheehan's **Heidegger: The Man and the Thinker** (Precedent, Chicago, 1981).

Selected texts by Heidegger:

1924: **The Concept of Time** (Blackwell, Oxford and Cambridge, Mass., 1992).

1927: **Being and Time**, tr. Joan Stambaugh (New York State University Press, 1996); also tr. John Macquarrie, Edward Robinson (Harper & Row, New York, 1962).

1930/1943: **"On the Essence of Truth"**, in Werner Brock (ed.), *Heidegger: Existence and Being* (Vision Press, London, and Regnery, Chicago, 1949).

1935-6: **"The Origin of the Work of Art"**, in David Farrell Krell (ed.), *Martin Heidegger: Basic Writings* (Routledge, London, and HarperCollins, New York, rev. edn. 1993).

1944: **"Remembrance of the Poet"**, and 1936: **"Hölderlin and the Essence of Poetry"**, in *Existence and Being*, above.

1946: **"Letter on Humanism"**, in *Basic Writings*, above.

1950-4: **Early Greek Thinking** (Harper & Row, New York, 1975).

1951: **"Building Dwelling Thinking"**, in *Basic Writings*, above.

1953: **"The Question Concerning Technology"**, in *Basic Writings*, above.

1955-7: **The Principle of Reason** (Indiana University Press, Bloomington, 1991).

1959: **On the Way To Language** (Harper & Row, New York, 1971).

For further reading:

The classic introductory essay is George Steiner's **Heidegger** (Fontana, London, and HarperCollins, New York, 1978, rev. edn. 1992). Walter Biemel's **Martin Heidegger: an Illustrated Study**, 1973 (Routledge & Kegan Paul, London, 1977, and Harcourt Brace Jovanovich, New York, 1976) is more detailed and carefully orthodox. A useful short guide to *Being and Time* is Stephen Mulhall's **Heidegger and "Being and Time"** (Routledge, London and New York, 1996).

For a sampling of recent Heidegger criticism, see **Heidegger: a Critical Reader**, ed. Hubert Dreyfus and Harrison Hall (Blackwell, Oxford and Cambridge, Mass., 1992), and **The Cambridge Companion to Heidegger**, ed. Charles Guignon (Cambridge University Press, Cambridge and New York, 1993). The latter has introductory essays and bibliographical references to many aspects of Heidegger's work.

On Heidegger's politics, see Richard Wolin (ed.), **The Heidegger Controversy** (MIT Press, Cambridge, Mass., 1993), and Hans Sluga, **Heidegger's Crisis: Philosophy and Politics in Nazi Germany** (Harvard University Press, Cambridge, Mass., 1993). The most substantial documentation is Hugo Ott's **Martin Heidegger: A Political Life**, 1988, (Fontana, London, 1994 and HarperCollins, New York, 1993).

The theological debates are introduced by John Macquarrie in **An Existentialist Theology** (Penguin, Harmondsworth, 1973). On Taoist and Buddhist influences, see Reinhard May, **Heidegger's Hidden Sources** (Routledge, London and New York, 1996).

Useful introductions to European Philosophy are Jenny Teichman and Graham White's **An Introduction to Modern European Philosophy** (Macmillan Press, Basingstoke, and St. Martin's Press, New York, 1995), and David West's **An Introduction to Continental Philosophy** (Polity Press, Cambridge, and Blackwell, Cambridge, Mass., 1996).

References

Page 16, Rainer Maria Rilke, "Concerning the Poet", in *Rodin and Other Prose Pieces*, ed. W. Tucker, tr. G. Houston (Quartet Books, 1986).

Page 112, Paul Celan, "Todtnauberg", in *Selected Poems*, tr. Michael Hamburger (Penguin, 1990).

Acknowledgements

The author would like to thank the many people who contributed to the production of this book, and especially, for loan of materials and other help, Michael Brook, Jo Gamble, John Giusti, Paul Lawley, Susan Purdie, Mike Roker, Anne Schneider and Philip Terry.

Jeff Collins trained as a fine artist and studied art history at the University of Leeds. He is currently a lecturer in Art History at the University of Plymouth, and writes and lectures on critical theory and contemporary culture. He is also the author of the introductory guide to Derrida in this series.

Howard Selina studied painting at St. Martins and the Royal Academy. He works in London as a painter and illustrator, and has exhibited in London and abroad.

Index